EASY GERMAN PHRASE BOOK

Over 1500 Common Phrases
For Everyday Use And Travel

www.LingoMastery.com

ISBN: 978-1-951949-16-7

Copyright © 2020 by Lingo Mastery

Free Book Reveals the 6-Step Blueprint That Took Students **from Language Learners to Fluent in 3 Months**

- **6 Unbelievable Hacks** that will accelerate your learning curve

- **Mind Training:** why memorizing vocabulary is easy

- **One Hack to Rule Them All:** This secret nugget will blow you away...

Head over to **LingoMastery.com/hacks**
and claim your free book now!

CONTENTS

INTRODUCTION

If you have finally decided to visit a German-speaking country, countries rich in history and culture, you may want to consider the words and phrases that might be of use in certain situations. English is the second language people learn at school in these countries, so you should be able to get through well with English, especially in the cities. In the countryside, however, or with older people, you'll be thankful for possessing at least basic-level German language skills.

Thanks to this book, we will see how to deal with many situations that can be simple, complicated, funny, or even not funny at all – all those real situations that a tourist will experience when, for example, they are seeking activities to do, order a perfectly cooked *Schweinsbraten* in a restaurant, or simply don't want to be bothered.

Think of the souvenirs to bring back to a relative. Do you want to negotiate on the price or ask for a discount? It is certainly here that you will need to find the way to express yourself correctly.

Most of the time, a translation with the vocabulary at your fingertips is the best solution, and therefore, why not take precautions and study a few phrases that could amaze your fellow travelers or your interlocutors?

Of course, there are some obstacles to overcome. Let's see, for example, what can create difficulties at a phonetic level in the German language.

Pronunciation of German vowels

There are 5 basic vowels in the German language: A, E, I, O, U.

The vowel A

'A' is usually pronounced similar to the 'a' in the English word 'car', not like in 'apple'. Unlike in English, the vowel 'A' in German doesn't usually change its pronunciation, so if you find an 'A' somewhere in a German sentence (even at the beginning of a word), you should be good to go if you use the 'a'-sound of the 'car'-word. For this book, simply think of every 'A' you encounter in a German word as this pronunciation. This is even true if you have a double 'A' in a word, like in the words 'Aal' (eel) or 'Saatgut' (seedlings). In these cases, simply prolong the sound a bit than you would with a single 'A'. Simple, right?

Ananas (pineapple), *AN-an-as*
// same as you would pronounce in English but remember to use the 'car'-Version of the vowel, even when the 'A' is at the start of the word.

Vater (father), *FAH-ter*
// V translates to F in pronunciation, stress the first part, the 't' is pronounced sharply, as in the English word 'track'

Hand (the hand), *HA-nd*
// same as in English but remember to use the 'car'-Version of the vowel!

Daten (data), *DAH-ten*
// use our German 'a'-Version found in 'car' again, for the 'e' use the version you can find in the English word 'get'

alt (old), *A-lt*
// watch to use the German 'a'-Version

The vowel E

'E', similar to 'A', is very easy to remember in English, since it doesn't change its pronunciation by itself. It's pronounced similar to the 'e' to be found in the English words 'get' or 'set'.

However, if this vowel is combined with other vowels directly next to each other, the sound will in most cases change. We'll come to that a bit later. If you find an 'e'-vowel without other vowels next to it (or 'eh'), you can be fairly sure to pronounce it correctly if you remember the word 'get'.

Elefant (elephant), *ele-FANT*

besser (better), *BE-sser*
// pronounced similar to English pronunciation, just watch to use the

'e' in 'get'

Internet (internet), *IN-ter-net*
// similar to English pronunciation, but watch to use the 'e' in 'get'

The vowel I

The vowel 'I' is pronounced similar to the 'I' in the English word 'fin'. This can be confusing at first for English language speakers because they are very used to pronounce the 'I' similar to the 'I' found in words like 'island'. Moreover, 'I' can be long or short in German. A long pronunciation can be the result of a combination with another vowel or consonant (we'll come to that later), but not necessarily so. Examples of the long version include:

Ihre (their) EE-re
Igel (hedgehog) EE-gel
Krise (crisis) KREE-se.

A short German 'I' can be found in words like :

Kind (child), KIND
finden (to find), *FIN-den*
Insel (island), *IN-sel*

The vowel O

Similarly, there are a long and a short version of 'O' in German. The long 'O' sounds similar to the English one in "go" or "old" but without gliding into a 'u'-sound at the end:

Ofen (oven), *OH-fen*
Rose (rose), *ROH-se*
Oma (grandmother), *OH-ma*

The short version of the 'O'-sound is like in English 'hot' or 'not':

Donner (thunder), *DO-ner*
hoffen (to hope), *HO-fen*

The vowel U

The German pronunciation of the vowel 'U' is different from the English one. The closest in the English language is probably the double-o in 'foot' or the 'u' in 'push'. In the following examples, try pronouncing each 'U' with no other vowels around it like you would pronounce the double o in 'foot'. Alright? Let's try:

Mund (mouth), *MU-nd*
// remember to make it a 'half-oo' with all the examples

unser (our), *UN-ser*

Bus (bus), *BUS*

Again, there is a distinction between a long and a short 'U' in German. While the previous examples were all short, a long "U" sounds like the double-o in 'root' or 'moon', just as in these examples:

Tuch (cloth), *TOOKH*
Stuhl (chair), *SHTOOL*

Ä, Ö; Ü (called 'Umlaute' in German)

In German you have several extra-vowels you don't find in the English language called 'Umlaute':

Ä

The 'Ä' is pretty similar to the 'a' pronounced the English way in 'apple'.

wählen (to vote), *VAEH-len*
// here the 'Ä'-sound is prolonged a bit by the 'H'-letter, see next chapter for notes on vowels followed by an 'H'.

ändern (to change), *AEN-dern*

Ö

The 'Ö' is a bit difficult to pronounce, because there are few similar sounds in English (the 'i' in 'flirt', or the 'o' in 'worm' come to mind), but you can do it. Start by pronouncing 'day' and keep voicing the last part of it. While you do, try to round your lips like you would when pronouncing an 'O'-sound, but keep your tongue and palate in the 'ay'-position. Perhaps a mirror might help you to get it right.

Öl (oil), *OE-L*

nötig (necessary), *NOE-tig*
// Note: an '-ig' in the ending of a word is always pronounced like the German 'ch' as in ich (I), ikh

Ü

Probably the most difficult is the 'Ü'-sound. You can start with the German 'I' (or English 'ee' like in 'meet') and then purse your lips until the sound changes. There's a German word with an 'Ü' in it you might have heard before, it's called 'über' (above) which has been translated to English as 'ueber'. It's often used in computer games for describing a very strong tool (like an 'ueber'-weapon as the strongest and most unfair one).

günstig (cheap), *GUENS-tig*
düster (dark), *DUE-ster*

Note: Sometimes if those vowels are not available (in certain fonts they aren't) they can also be written with their vowel-brothers followed by an 'E'. So, an 'Ä' becomes 'AE', an 'Ö' becomes 'OE' and an 'Ü' becomes 'UE'. If you take 'Österreich' (Austria) for example, it's sometimes written as 'Oesterreich' instead.

Pronunciation of vowels with an 'H' after them

In many cases, you'll find a vowel followed by an 'H' and then a consonant in the German language, like in 'Mehl' (flour). In most cases, the 'H' after the vowel will simply prolong the vowel for a bit. So, in case of 'Mehl' the length of the 'e' sound is longer. Easy, right? So, let's try that with a few examples:

Zahlen (numbers), *TSAH-len*
// the 'Z' sound is pronounced like a very strong 'TS' sound, like you would take a strong 'T' and then add the beginning of the word 'zoom' after that. The 'ts' in the word 'cats' comes close, or the 'ts' in 'lots of'.

Uhr (clock), *OOR*

ohne (without), *OH-ne*

zählen (to count), *TSAEH-len*

// pronounce the 'z' as you would pronounce a strong 'ts'. And yes, Ä/Ö/Ü can be prolonged by an 'H' as well.

Note: You won't find a German word with an 'I' followed by an 'H' where the 'I' is prolonged by that. There's a special diphthong for this case, which is written a little bit differently, see 'IE'.

The following pronouns are exceptions to this: Ihn (*EEN*), Ihnen (*EE-nen*), Ihr (*EER*), Ihre (*EE-re*), Ihren (*EE-ren*), Ihrem (*EE-rem*), Ihm (*EEM*)

The 'Y' (epsilon, or 'Ypsilon' in German)

In German the 'Y' is used either similarly to 'Ü', like in the German word 'Thymian' (thyme), or it sometimes is used as a 'I', like in 'Playstation', especially when Germans pronounce words that were taken from foreign languages.

Xylophon (xylophone), *KSUE-lo-FON*
// here the 'Y' is pronounced as a 'Ü', and the 'PH' is pronounced as 'F' (see consonants for an explanation)

Yoga (yoga), *YO-ga*
*// here the 'Y' is pronounced similarly to a German 'I' or a 'J', they sound very similar in German at times. **Note**: sometimes they spell it 'Joga' in German, too*

Baby (baby), *BAY-bee*
// here again the 'Y' is pronounced as an 'I'. The 'a' is pronounced similarly to the 'a' in the English word 'amen' to make it more similar to the English pronunciation where German lent the word from.

Pronunciation of German diphthongs

There are quite a few diphthongs in the German language. Let's start with the easy ones: 'ei', 'ai'and ie'.

'EI' and 'AI'

The diphthongs 'ei' and 'ai' are pronounced as you would expect when you combine a German 'A' with a German 'I' without thinking it through, so the result is something similar to the 'I' in the English word 'ice'.

Now what's the difference between 'ai' and 'ei' then? In most words, you won't hear the difference at all, because the difference is mostly a remnant of old times where you would have different spellings for similar sounds in different German regions. For some words, though, the 'A' sound in the 'ai' diphthong is pronounced with just a little bit more force than in the 'ei' diphthong. If you want to impress someone, you can follow that rule of thumb. But even German people often interchange the two sounds when they pronounce them.

Reise (journey), *RIGH-se*
einkaufen (to shop), *IGHN-kau-fen*
Laib (loaf of bread), *LIGHB*

The diphthong 'IE' (also called 'Langes I' or 'long I')

This one works similar to a vowel with an 'H' afterwards. An 'IE' is simply a German 'I' that is prolonged a bit more. For example, if you have the word 'biegen' (to bend), the 'ie' sound is simply a very long German 'I'-sound, similar to the 'ee' in 'meet'.

nie (never), *nee*
Liebe (love), *LEE-be*
sie (she), *SEE*

The diphthongs 'AU' and 'EU'

The 'AU'-sound is very simple, too: Just combine a German 'a' with a German 'u' (remember, imagine a shortened vowel of 'moon' for the German 'u'!). A wonderful example is the German word 'Maus' ('mouse'), because although the words are written differently, they are pronounced very similarly. The 'ou' sound in 'mouse' sounds exactly like the 'au' sound in German you're aiming for. Same for 'house', so imagining the English 'ou' sound should help you.

Haus (house), *HAUS*
bauen (to build), *BAU-en*
Mauer (wall), *MAU-er*

The 'EU'-sound is also quite easy to pronounce if you take the English word 'oyster' as a reference. The 'oy' in 'oyster' is exactly what you're aiming for. Now try it with the German word 'neu' (new). Easy, right?

neu (new), *NOY*

teuer (expensive), *TOY-er*
Feuer (fire), *FOY-er*

German consonants

Similar consonants in German and English

There are several consonants which in General are used in German in a similar way as you would use them in English. This applies to: **b, d, f, g, k, l, m, n, p, q, r, s, t, x.**

Sometimes several similar ones of these are written next to each other, like in 'Ebbe' (ebb, of ebb and flow) or 'Kamm' (comb). Those are easy to pronounce, though, because they often serve to shorten the preceding sound (mostly a vowel sound). In some other cases it might sound like you can actually hear the consonant two times. You can try it out yourself with some examples:

Neffe (nephew), NE-fe

hatte (he had), *HA-te*

erkennen (to recognize), *er-KEN-nen*

kommen (to come), *KOM-men*

German consonants that work differently than in English

There are many consonants in the German language that are quite similar to the English ones, but there are also a few special ones you might want to look out for. Let's start with the most confusing one: ß.

ß

The 'ß'-sound is also called 'Scharfes S' in German, or 'sharp s'. It is quite rare in the German language, and if you find it in a word, you'll usually find it after a dipththong, like in 'gießen' (to water). It is pronounced like a normal 's', but you prolong it a bit (similar like 'AH' creates a longer 'A' sound). For this book, every time you see a 'ß' think of a long but usually soft 's'-sound.

heiß (hot), *HIGHSS*
beißen (to bite), *BIGH-ssen*

fließen (to flow), FLEE-ssen

In the rare cases where it doesn't follow a diphthong, it does sometimes prolong the vowel before it a bit, too, like in 'aß' (he ate), there you would pronounce it something like 'ahs', with a prolonged 'A'.

fraß (it ate, but for animals), *frah-s*

Combined consonants in English pronounced differently in German

In English there are several consonants that are pronounced a certain way, for example the 'TH'-consonant, which doesn't exist in German as it does in English.

TH

There is no English 'TH' sound in German. Instead, a simple combination of a 'T' with a German 'H' (as in 'Hi') is used whenever you spot a 'TH' letter combination.

Thailand (Thailand*), T-HIGH-land*
Thymian (thyme), *T-HUE-mi-an*

PH

The 'PH'-sound becomes an 'F'-sound in German, as in 'far'. It's not very common to spot an 'PH'-spelling in German words, for in most cases it has already been exchanged for the 'F'-spelling. But if you pronounce it as you would in English, you're fine.

Phantasie (phantasy), *Fan-ta-SEE*
Phiole (vial), *Fi-OH-le*
Paragraph (paragraph), *Pa-ra-GRAHF*

J

The 'J'-letter in English isn't pronounced similarly in German. If you pronounce the word 'year', the 'y' sound is what you're aiming for in a German 'j'.

Jahr (year), *YAHR*
Ja (yes), *YAH*
Japan (Japan), *YAH-pahn*

9

SH

The English 'SH' doesn't exist in the German spelling, but the sound does. It's written "sch" instead (see 'SCH').

ST

The 'ST' consonant pair sounds like it does in English, except if you find it at the beginning of a word. In this case you have to substitute an English "SH"-sound for the 'S', so it becomes an English "SHT". This is also true when a word beginning with 'ST' is used as the final element in a compound word:

Hauptstadt (capital city) *HAUPT-shtat*
Stahl (steel), *SHTAHL*
Stern (star), *SHTERN*
Stufe (step), *SHTOO-fe*

SP

Same as with 'ST', the 'SP' consonant pair will be pronounced as 'SHP' if it is at the start of a word. This is also true when a word beginning with 'SP' is used as the final element in a compound word. If it is anywhere else, it stays as it is.

Ballspiel (ball game) *BALL-shpeel*
sparen (to save money), *shp-AHR-en*
sprechen (to speak), *shp-REKH-en*
Sprache (language), *Shp-RAKH-e*

Special consonants in German (that are pronounced differently than in English)

C

Let's start with the easy ones. First one is 'C'. This one doesn't really exist on its own, usually it only exists as a combined consonant (see combined consonants).

H

Next one is 'H'. We already covered 'H' when it is following a vowel (in this case it prolongs it). It can be part of a combined consonant (see combined consonant). Or it can be at the beginning of a word. In this case, it works exactly as it would in English, like in 'Hi' (German: 'Hallo').

V

Now for 'V', which is in most cases pronounced like an English 'F'. There are some loan words from other languages in which 'V' may be pronounced like an English 'V' (Vegetarier, *vay-ge-TAH-ree-er*), but chances are that the correct pronunciation is an 'F'-sound whenever you come across a German 'V'. There really are not many easy rules on when to use which pronunciation, often times you'll simply have to know for certain words. There's one easy to remember though: If a word starts with the word-part 'ver' (as in 'verkaufen' or 'verbieten'), you'll use the 'F'-sound.

W

The German 'W', on the other hand, is usually pronounced like an English 'V'.

> warten (to wait), *VAHR-ten*
> anwenden (to apply), *AN-ven-den*
> Löwe (lion), *LOEH-ve*

J

The 'J' consonant is pronounced like the English 'Y' in 'year', or in 'play'.

Z

The 'Z' consonant is pronounced similar to the English 'TS' found in 'cats' or 'lots of'.

Combined consonants in German

There are a few additional consonant-combinations you should be aware of.

CK

The easiest one is 'CK' because it also exists in the English language and is pronounced similarly, like in the English word 'track'. It's basically a forceful variation of the 'K' consonant.

SCH

Second one is 'SCH', which resembles the English 'SH' sound found in the word 'she' for example.

TSCH

Next is 'TSCH' which is the same as 'SCH', only there's a 'T' in front. If you pronounce the English word 'child', you can hear the correct pronunciation.

CH

The last and probably most difficult one is 'CH', because there is no real role model word in English. If you ever heard a cat hissing at a dog (* sound) or if you clear your throat (* sound) , then you're very close to how it sounds.

If you want to get close, pronouncing it yourself , you have to consider two ways of pronunciation, either when combined with a, o , u, au or in combination with e, i, ai, ei, eu.

For the first way (when combined with a, o , u, au), you can start out with forming a soft 'K' sound in your mouth and try to make it longer. Don't repeat it but prolong it: "khhhhh" (* sound)

The second way (when combined with e, i, ai, ei, eu) is like a whispered "yyyyyes". Again: don't just repeat it, but prolong it.

If you do it right, it should sound a bit like a hissing cat. (*sound)

Here are a few example words for you to practice this difficult double consonant:

danach (later), da-NAHKH

Loch (hole), *Lokh*

echt (real), *ekht*

ich (I), ikh

Ich liebe dich (I love you), *Ikh LEE-be dikh*
// Throughout this book we use the phonetic spelling "kh" for both variations

Bonus notes on dialects

In certain areas of Germany, Switzerland and especially Austria there are certain dialects that might make it hard to understand what someone is saying. Usually people are able to speak 'Hochdeutsch' (standard German) if needed, but especially in rural areas you might encounter people who are so used to using their dialect instead that they forgot how to speak 'Hochdeutsch'.

Since dialects are numerous, it's impossible to give you a complete overview of what might change in these dialects and why. Often times, certain vowels are not pronounced or will change their sound. For example, it's very common in certain Austrian dialects to not pronounce the last 'E' of any word ending with 'ER' or 'EN', or exchange that 'E' vowel for an 'A' vowel. If what you hear really confuses you, you might want to ask if someone would be kind enough to speak 'Hochdeusch' (standard German) with you. Most people will be very understanding and gladly try their best to make themselves more comprehensible.

Here are some Austrian slang wordswhich you might be able to impress the locals with (pronunciation descriptions are based on the German pronunciation rules covered above):

Eichhörnchenschwanz (tail of a squirrel), *OAKH-katsl-shwOAF*
// *This is a word most locals LOVE to ask strangers to pronounce*

Schweinebraten (roast pork), *SHWIGHNS-brodn*
// *You SHOULD taste this, it's really good!*

herauf (up), *AU-fi*

Komm schon, lass uns gehen! (Come on, let's go!), *KOMM-sho GEH-ma!*

Komm herüber (come over), *KOMM OOM-ee*

Du and Sie: a note about the German way of addressing people

As in many European countries, German-speakers tend to be formal and reserved when conducting their personal and business affairs. There is both an informal and a formal form of "you": du (doo) and Sie (See). The formal "Sie" (capitalized!) creates a sense of respect or distance while the familiar "du" creates a sense of intimacy and familiarity.

As both the informal "du" and the formal "Sie" are used frequently in German language this book will provide examples of both forms. Depending on the situation and the relationship between conversational partners it could be more appropriate to use the other form as the one provided in a sample. Any of the sentences in this book could be said either way.

For example, "Where do you live?" can be said using both forms:

Du: "Wo wohnst du?" (*Vo vohnst doo?)*

Sie: "Wo wohnen Sie?" (*Vo VOH-nen See?*)

COLORS

Gold
Gold
Gold
// The 'o' is similar to the 'o' in 'of'

Red
Rot
Roht

Orange
Orange
Oh-RAHGSH

Yellow
Gelb
Gelb

Green
Grün
Gruen

Blue
Blau
Blau

Light blue
Hellblau
HELL-blau

Violet
Violett
Vee-o-LETT

Pink
Rosa
ROH-sa

Brown
Braun
Braun

Purple
Lila
LEE-la

White
Weiß
VIGHSS

Black
Schwarz
SHVARTS

Gray
Grau
Grau

Silver
Silber
SIL-ber

What color is that sign?
Welche Farbe hat dieses Zeichen?
VEL-khe FAR-be hat DEE-ses TSIGH-khen?

Is the cartoon in color?
Ist der Cartoon in Farbe?
Ist der Car-TOON in FAR-be?

Is this television show in color?
Ist diese Fernsehshow in Farbe?
Ist DEE-se FERN-say-show in FAR-be?

This is a red pen.
Das ist ein roter Stift.
Das ist ighn ROH-ter Shtift.

This piece of paper is blue.
Dieses Blatt Papier ist blau.
DEE-ses Blatt Pa-PEER ist blau.

What color is that car?
Welche Farbe hat das Auto?
VEL-khe FAR-be hat das AU-to?

What color are your clothes?
Welche Farbe hat deine Kleidung?
VEL-khe FAR-be hat DIGH-ne KLIGH-dung?

Is this the right color?
Ist das die richtige Farbe?
Ist das dee RIKH-ti-ge FAR-be?

What color is the stop light?
Welche Farbe hat die Ampel?
VEL-khe FAR-be hat dee AM-pel?

Does that color mean danger?
Bedeutet diese Farbe Gefahr?
Be-DOY-tet DEE-se FAR-be Ge-FAHR?

That bird is red.
Dieser Vogel ist rot.
DEE-ser FO-gel ist roht.

What color is that animal?
Welche Farbe hat das Tier?
VEL-che FAR-be hat das TEER?

The sky is blue.
Der Himmel ist blau.
Der HIM-mel ist blau.

The clouds are white.
Die Wolken sind weiß.
Dee WOL-ken sind vighss.

That paint is blue.
Diese Farbe ist blau.
DEE-se FAR-be ist blau.

Press the red button.
Drücke den roten Knopf.
DRUE-kke den ROH-ten KNOPF.

Don't press the red button.
Drücke den roten Knopf nicht.
DRUE-kke den ROH-ten Knopf NIKHT.

Black and White
Schwarz und weiß
SHVARTS und VIGHSS

Look at all the colors.
Schau dir all die Farben an.
Shau deer all dee FAR-ben an.

Is that a color television?
Ist das ein Farbfernseher?
Ist das ighn FARB-fern-se-her?

What color do you see?
Welche Farbe siehst du?
VEL-khe FAR-be seehst doo?

Can I have the color blue?
Kann ich die Farbe Blau haben?
Kann ikh die FAR-be Blau HA-ben?

What colors do you have for these frames?
Welche Farben haben Sie für den Rahmen?
VEL-khe FAR-ben HA-ben See fuer den RAH-men?

Don't go until the color is green.
Geh nicht, bis die Farbe grün ist.
Geh nikht, bis dee FAR-be gruen ist.

Colored pencils
Farbstifte
FAR-shtiff-te

Coloring pens
Malstifte
MAHL-shtiff-te

The sharpie is black.
Der Edding ist schwarz
Der EH-ding ist shvarts

Do you have this in another color?
Haben Sie das auch in einer anderen Farbe?
HAH-ben See das aukh in IGH-ner AN-der-en FAR-be?

Do you have this in a darker color?
Haben Sie das auch in einer dunkleren Farbe?
HAH-ben See das aukh in IGH-ner DOONG-kler-en FAR-be?

Do you have this in a lighter color?
Haben Sie das auch in einer helleren Farbe?
HAH-ben See das aukh in IGH-ner HELLI-er-en FAR-be?

Can you paint my house blue?
Können Sie mein Haus blau streichen?
KOEN-nen See mighn Haus blau SHTRIGH-khen?

Can you paint my car the same color?
Können Sie mein Auto mit derselben Farbe lackieren?
KOEN-nen See mighn AU-to mitt der-SELL-ben FAR-be la-KEE-ren?

The flag has three different colors.
Die Flagge hat drei verschiedene Farben.
Dee FLA-gge hat drigh fer-SHEE-de-ne FAR-ben.

Is the color on the flag red?
Ist die Farbe der Flagge rot?
Ist dee FAR-be der FLA-gge roht?

NUMBERS

Zero
Null
Null

One
Eins
IGHns

Two
Zwei
Tsvigh

Three
Drei
Drigh

Four
Vier
Feer

Five
Fünf
Fuenf

Six
Sechs
Sekhs

Seven
Sieben
See-ben

Eight
Acht
Akht

Nine
Neun
Noyn

Ten
Zehn
Tsayn

Eleven
Elf
Elf

Twelve
Zwölf
Tsvoelf

Thirteen
Dreizehn
DRIGH-tsayn

Fourteen
Vierzehn
Feer-tsayn

Fifteen
Fünfzehn
Fuenf-tsayn

Sixteen
Sechzehn
Sekh-tsayn

Seventeen
Siebzehn
Seeb-tsayn

Eighteen
Achtzehn
Akht-tsayn

Nineteen
Neunzehn
Noyn-tsayn

Twenty
Zwanzig
TSVAHN-tsig

Twenty-one
Einundzwanzig
IGHN-oond-tsvahn-tsig

Twenty-two
Zweiundzwanzig
TSVIGH-oond-tsvahn-tsig

Twenty-three
Dreiundzwanzig
DRIGH-oond-tsvahn -tsig

Twenty-four
Vierundzwanzig
FEER-oond-tsvahn-tsig

Twenty-five
Fünfundzwanzig
FUENF-oond-tsvahn-tsig

Twenty-six
Sechsundzwanzig
SEKHS-oond-tsvahn-tsig

Twenty-seven
Siebenundzwanzig
SEE-ben-oond-tsvahn-tsig

Twenty-eight
Achtundzwanzig
AKHT-oond-tsvahn-tsig

Twenty-nine
Neunundzwanzig
NOYN-oond-tsvahn-tsig

Thirty
Dreißig
DRIGH-ssig

Forty
Vierzig
FEER-tsig

Fifty
Fünfzig
FUENF-tsig

Sixty
Sechzig
SEKH-tsig

Seventy
Siebzig
SEEB-tsig

Eighty
Achtzig
AKHT-tsig

Ninety
Neunzig
NOYN-tsig

One hundred
Hundert
HOON-dert

Two hundred
Zweihundert
TSVIGH-hoon-dert

Five hundred
Fünfhundert
FUENF-hoon-dert

One thousand
Tausend
TAU-send

One hundred thousand
Hunderttausend
HOON-dert-tau-send

One million
Eine Million
IGH-ne Mil-li-OHN

One billion
Eine Milliarde
IGH-ne Mil-li-AR-de

What does that add up to?
Was macht das im Ganzen?
Vahs makht das im GAN-tsen?

What number is on this paper?
Welche Zahl ist auf diesem Papier?
VEL-khe Tsahl ist auf DEE-sem Pa-PEER?

What number is on this sign?
Welche Zahl ist auf diesem Zeichen?
VEL-che TSAHL ist auf DEE-sem TSIGH-khen?

Are these two numbers equal?
Sind diese beiden Zahlen gleich?
Sind DEE-se BIGH-den TSAH-len glighkh?

My social security number is one, two, three, four, five.
Meine Sozialversicherungsnummer ist eins, zwei, drei, vier, fünf.
MIGH-ne So-tsi-AHL-fer-SIKHER-ungs-NU-mer ist ighns, tsvigh, drigh, feer, fuenf.

I'm going to bet five hundred euros.
Ich wette um fünfhundert Euro.
Ikh VET-te um FUENF-hoon-dert OY-ro.

Can you count to one hundred for me?
Kannst du für mich bis hundert zählen?
Kannst doo fuer mich bis HOON-dert TSAEH-len?

I took fourteen steps.
Ich habe vierzehn Schritte gemacht.
Ikh HAH-be FEER-tsayn SHRI-te ge-MAKHT.

I ran two kilometers.
Ich rannte zwei Kilometer.
Ikh RAN-te tsvigh KIL-o-may-ter.

The speed limit is 30 km/h.
Die Geschwindigkeitsbeschränkung ist 30 km/h.
Dee Ge-SHVIN-dig-kights-be-SHRAEN-kung ist 30 km/h.

What are the measurements?
Wie sind die Abmessungen?
Vee sind dee AB-mes-sung-en?

Can you dial this number?
Kannst du diese Nummer wählen?
Kannst doo DEE-se NU-mer waeh-len?

One dozen.
Ein Dutzend.
Ighn DU-tsend.

A half-dozen.
Ein halbes Dutzend.
Ighn HAL-bes DU-tsend.

How many digits are in the number?
Wie viele Ziffern sind in dieser Zahl?
Vee FEE-le TSI-fern sind in DEE-ser Tsahl?

My phone number is nine, eight, five, six, two, one, eight, seven, eight, eight.

Meine Telefonnummer ist neun, acht, fünf, sechs, zwei, eins, acht, sieben, acht, acht.

MIGH-ne Te-le-FOHN-nu-mer ist noyn, akht, fuenf, sekhs, tsvigh, ighns, akht, SEE-ben, akht, akht.

The hotel's phone number is one, eight hundred, three, two, three, five, seven, five, five.

Die Telefonnummer des Hotels ist eins, achthundert, drei, zwei, drei, fünf, sieben, fünf, fünf.

Dee Te-le-FOHN-nu-mer des Ho-TELLS ist ighns, akgt-HOON-dert, drigh, tsvigh, drigh, fuenf, SEE-ben, fuenf, fuenf.

The taxi number is six, eight, one, four, four, four, five, eight, one, nine.

Die Nummer des Taxis ist sechs, acht, eins, vier, vier, vier, fünf, acht, eins, neun.

Dee NU-mer des TAK-sees ist sekhs, akht, ighns, feer, feer, feer, fuenf, akht, ighns, noyn.

Call my hotel at two, one, four, seven, one, two, nine, five, seven, six.

Rufen Sie mein Hotel an unter zwei, eins, vier, sieben, eins, zwei, neun, fünf, sieben, sechs.

ROO-fen See mighn Ho-TEL an UN-ter tsvigh, ighns, feer, SEE-ben, ighns, tsvigh, noyn, fuenf, SEE-ben, sekhs.

Call the embassy at nine, eight, nine, eight, four, three, two, one, seven, one.

Rufen Sie die Botschaft an unter neun, acht, neun, acht, vier, drei, zwei, eins, sieben, eins.

ROO-fen See dee BOHT-shaft an UN-ter noyn, akht, noyn, akht, feer, drigh, tsvigh, ighns, SEE-ben, ighns.

GREETINGS

Hi!
Hallo!
HA-lo!

How's it going?
Wie geht's?
Vee GAYTS?

What's new?
Was gibt's Neues?
Vas geebts NOY-es?

What's going on?
Was ist los?
Vahs ist LOHS?

Home, sweet home.
Endlich zuhause.
END-likh tsoo-HAU-se.

Ladies and gentlemen, thank you for coming.
Meine Damen und Herren, danke fürs Kommen.
Migh-ne DAH-men und HE-ren, DAN-ke fuers KOM-men.

How is everything?
Wie geht es dir?
Vee GAYT es deer?

Long time, no see.
Lange nicht gesehen.
LAN-ge nikht ge-SAY-hen.

It's been a long time.
Es ist lange her.
Es ist LAN-ge hayr.

It's been a while!
Es ist eine ganze Weile her.
Es ist igh-ne GAN-tse VIGH-le hayr.

How is life?
Wie ist dein Leben so verlaufen?
Vee ist dighn LAY-ben so fer-LAU-fen?

How is your day?
Wie ist dein Tag?
Vee ist dighn Tahg?

Good morning.
Guten Morgen.
GOO-ten MOR-gen.

It's been too long!
Es ist zu lange her!
Es ist tsoo LAN-ge hayr!

Good afternoon.
Guten Nachmittag.
GOO-ten NAKH-mit-tahg.

How long has it been?
Wie lange ist es her?
Vee LAN-ge ist es hayr?

It's a pleasure to meet you.
Es ist mir eine Freude, Sie zu treffen.
Es ist meer igh-ne FROY-de, See tsoo TREF-fen.

It's always a pleasure to see you.
Es ist mir immer eine Freude, dich zu sehen.
Es ist meer IM-mer igh-ne FROY-de dikh tsoo SAY-hen

Allow me to introduce Earl, my husband.
Erlaube mir, dir meinen Mann Earl vorzustellen.
Er-LAU-be meer, deer MIGH-nen Mann Earl FOR-tsoo-shtel-len.

Goodnight.
Gute Nacht.
GOO-te Nakht.

May I introduce my brother and sister?
Darf ich dir meinen Bruder und meine Schwester vorstellen?
Darf ikh deer migh-nen BROO-der und migh-ne SHVES-ter FOR-shtel-len?

Good evening.
Guten Abend.
GOO-ten AH-bend.

What's happening?
Was ist passiert?
Vas ist pa-SEERT?

Happy holidays!
Schöne Feiertage!
SHOE-ne FIGH-er-tah-ge!

Are you alright?
Alles in Ordnung?
AL-les in ORD-noong?

Merry Christmas!
Frohe Weihnachten!
FROH-he VIGH-nakh-ten!

Where have you been hiding?
Wo hast du dich versteckt?
Voh hast doo dikh fer-SHTEKKT?

Happy New Year!
Gutes Neues Jahr!
GOO-tes NOY-es YAHR!

How is your night?
Wie ist dein Abend?
Vee ist dighn Ah-bend?

What have you been up to all these years?
Was hast du all die Jahre gemacht?
Vas hast doo all dee YAH-re ge-MAKHT?

When was the last time we saw each other?
Wann haben wir uns das letzte Mal gesehen?
Vann HA-ben veer uns das LETS-te Mahl ge-SAY-hen?

It's been ages since I've seen you.
Es ist so lange her, dass wir uns gesehen haben.
Es ist so LAN-ge her, dass veer uns ge-SAY-hen HAH-ben.

How have things been going since I saw you last?
Was ist passiert, seit wir uns das letzte Mal gesehen haben?
Vas ist pa-SEERT, sight veer uns das LETS-te Mahl ge-SAY-hen HAH-ben?

What have you been up to?
Was hast du in der Zwischenzeit gemacht?
Vas hast doo in der TSVISH-en-tsight ge-MAKHT?

How are you doing?
Wie geht's?
Vee GAYTS?

Goodbye.
Auf Wiedersehen.
Auf VEE-der-say-hen.

Are you okay?
Alles ok bei dir?
AL-les o-KAY bigh deer?

How's life been treating you?
Wie ist es dir ergangen?
Vee ist es deer er-GANG-en?

I'm sorry.
Es tut mir leid.
Es toot meer LIGHD.

Excuse me.
Entschuldigen Sie.
Ent-SHOOL-di-gen See.

See you later!
Bis später!
Bis SHPAE-ter!

What's your name?
Wie ist dein Name?
Vee ist dighn NAH-me ?

My name is Bill.
Mein Name ist Bill.
Mighn NAH-me ist Bill.

Pleased to meet you.
Freut mich, Sie kennenzulernen.
Froyt mikh See KEN-nen-tsoo-LER-nen.

How do you do?
Wie geht es Ihnen?
Vee gayt es EE-nen?

How are things?
Wie ist es gelaufen?
Vee ist es ge-LAU-fen?

You're welcome.
Keine Ursache.
KIGH-ne OOR-sakh-e.

It's good to see you.
Es ist gut, dich zu sehen.
Es ist goot deekh tsoo SAY-hen.

How have you been?
Wie ist es dir ergangen?
Vee ist es deer er-GAHNG-en?

Nice to meet you.
Schön, Sie kennenzulernen.
SHOEN, See KEN-nen-tsoo-LER-nen.

Fine, thanks. And you?
Gut, danke. Und Ihnen?
Goot, DAN-ke. Oond EE-nen?

Good day to you.
Einen guten Tag Ihnen.
IGH-nen GOO-ten Tahg EE-nen.

Come in, the door is open.
Kommen Sie herein, die Tür ist offen.
KOM-men See her-RIGHN, dee TUER ist OF-fen.

My wife's name is Sheila.
Der Name meiner Frau ist Sheila.
Der NAH-me MIGH-ner Frau ist Sheila.

I've been looking for you!
Ich habe nach dir gesucht!
Ikh HAH-be nakh deer ge-SOOKHT!

Allow me to introduce myself. My name is Earl.
Erlauben Sie mir, mich vorzustellen. Mein Name ist Earl.
Er-LAU-ben See meer, mikh FOR-tsoo-shtel-len. Mighn NAH-me ist Earl.

I hope you have enjoyed your weekend!
Ich hoffe, du hattest ein schönes Wochenende!
Ikh HO-fe, doo HA-test ighn SHOE-nes VOKH-en-en-de!

It's great to hear from you.
Es ist schön, von dir zu hören.
Es ist shoen, fon deer tsoo HOE-ren.

I hope you are having a great day.
Ich hoffe, du hast einen großartigen Tag.
Ikh HO-fe, doo hast igh-nen GROHSS-ar-tee-gen Tahg.

Thank you for your help.
Danke für Ihre Hilfe.
DAN-ke fuer EE-re HIL-fe.

DATE AND TIME

January
Januar
YA-noo-ar

February
Februar
FEH-broo-ar

March
März
Maerts

April
April
A-PRIL

May
Mai
Migh

June
Juni
YOO-nee

July
Juli
YOO-lee

August
August
Au-GOOST

September
September
Sep-TEM-ber

October
Oktober
Ok-TOH-ber

November
November
No-VEM-ber

December
Dezember
De-TSEM-ber

What month is it?
Welchen Monat haben wir?
VEL-khen MOH-nat HAH-ben veer?

At what time?
Zu welcher Zeit?
Tsoo VEL-kher Tsight?

Do you observe Daylight saving time?
Gibt es hier eine Zeitumstellung?
Geebt es heer IGH-ne TSIGHT-oom-shtel-loong?

The current month is January.
Der derzeitige Monat ist Januar.
Der DER-tsigh-tee-ge MOH-nat ist YAH-noo-ar.

What day of the week is it?
Welchen Wochentag haben wir?
VEL-khen VO-khen-tag HAH-ben veer?

Is today Tuesday?
Ist heute Dienstag?
Ist HOY-te DEENS-tahg?

Today is Monday.
Heute ist Montag.
HOY-te ist MOHN-tahg.

Is this the month of January?
Ist das der Monat Januar?
Ist das der MOH-nat YAH-noo-ar?

It is five minutes past one.
Es ist fünf nach eins.
Es ist fuenf nakh ighns.

It is ten minutes past one.
Es ist zehn nach eins.
Es ist tsayn nakh ighns .

It is ten till one.
Es ist zehn vor eins.
Es ist tsayn for ighns .

It is half past one.
Es ist halb zwei.
Es ist halb tsvigh.

What time is it?
Wie spät ist es?
Vee SHPAET ist es?

When does the sun go down?
Wann geht die Sonne unter?
Vann gayt dee SON-ne UN-ter?

It's the third of November.
Es ist der dritte November.
Es ist der DRI-te No-VEM-ber.

When does it get dark?
Wann wird es dunkel?
Vann vird es DUN-kel?

What is today's date?
Welches Datum haben wir heute?
VEL-khes DAH-tum HAH-ben veer hoy-te?

What time does the shoe store open?
Wann macht das Schuhgeschäft auf?
Vann makht das SHOO-ge-shaeft auf?

Is today a holiday?
Ist heute ein Feiertag?
Ist HOY-te ighn FIGH-er-tag?

When is the next holiday?
Wann sind die nächsten Ferien?
Vann sind dee NAEKH-sten FAYR-ee-en?

I will meet you at noon.
Ich werde dich zu Mittag treffen.
Ikh WAYR-de dikh tsoo MIT-tahg TREF-fen.

I will meet you later tonight.
Ich werde dich später am Abend treffen.
Ikh WAYR-de dikh SHPEA-ter am AH-bend TREF-fen.

My appointment is in ten minutes.
Meine Verabredung ist in zehn Minuten.
Migh-ne Fer-AB-ray-doong ist in tsayn Mee-NOO-ten.

Can we meet in half an hour?
Können wir uns in einer halben Stunde treffen?
KOEN-nen veer uns in igh-ner HAL-ben SHTOON-de TREF-fen?

I will see you in March.
Ich werde dich im März wiedersehen.
Ikh WAYR-de dikh im Maerts VEE-der-se-hen.

The meeting is scheduled for the twelfth.
Das Treffen ist für den Zwölften geplant.
Das TREF-fen ist fuer den TSVOELF-ten ge-PLAHNT.

Can we set up the meeting for noon tomorrow?
Können wir das Treffen für morgen Mittag ansetzen?
KOEN-nen veer das TREF-fen fuer MOR-gen MIT-tahg AN-se-tsen?

What time will the cab arrive?
Wann wird das Taxi ankommen?
Vann vird das TAK-see AN-kom-men?

Can you be here by midnight?
Kannst du bis Mitternacht hier sein?
Kannst doo bis MIT-ter-nakht heer sighn?

The grand opening is scheduled for three o'clock.
Die große Eröffnung ist für drei Uhr geplant.
Dee GROH-sse Er-OEFF-noong ist fuer DRIGH Oor ge-PLAHNT.

When is your birthday?
Wann hast du Geburtstag?
Vann hast doo Ge-BOORTS-tahg?

My birthday is on the second of June.
Mein Geburtstag ist am zweiten Juni.
Mighn Ge-BOORTS-tahg ist am TSVIGH-ten YOO-nee.

This place opens at ten a.m.
Diese Einrichtung öffnet um zehn Uhr morgens.
DEE-se IGHN-rikh-toong OEFF-net umm TSAYN Oor MOR-gens.

From what time?

Ab wie viel Uhr?

Ab vee feel Oor?

Sorry, it is already too late at night.

Tut mir leid, es ist schon zu spät in der Nacht.

Toot meer lighd, es ist shohn tsoo shpaet in der Nakht.

COMMON QUESTIONS

Do you speak English?
Sprechen Sie Englisch?
SHPRE-khen See ENG-lish?

What is your hobby?
Was sind deine Hobbys?
Vas sind DIGH-ne HOB-bees?

What language do you speak?
Welche Sprache sprechen Sie?
VEL-khe SHPRAH-khe SHPRE-khen See?

Was it hard?
War es schwierig?
Vahr es SHVEE-rig?

Can you help me?
Können Sie mir helfen?
KOEN-nen See meer HEL-fen?

Where can I find help?
Wer kann mir helfen?
Vehr kann meer HEL-fen?

Where are we right now?
Wo sind wir gerade?
Voh sind veer ge-RAH-de?

Where were you last night?
Wo warst du letzte Nacht?
Voh vahrst doo LET-ste Nakht?

What type of a tree is that?
Was für ein Baum ist das?
Vas fuer ighn Baum IST das?

Do you plan on coming back here again?
Willst du wieder hierher zurückkommen?
VILL-st doo VEE-der HEER-her tsoo-RUECK-kom-men?

What kind of an animal is that?
Welches Tier ist das?
VEL-ches Teer ist das?

Is that animal dangerous?
Ist dieses Tier gefährlich?
Ist DEES-es Teer ge-FAEHR-likh?

Is it available?
Ist es verfügbar?
Ist es fer-FUEG-bar?

Can we come see it?
Können wir es sehen?
KOEN-nen veer es SAY-hen?

Where do you live?
Wo wohnst du?
Voh vohnst doo?

Earl, what city are you from?
Earl, aus welcher Stadt bist du?
Earl, aus VEL-cher Shtatt bist doo?

Is it a very large city?
Ist das eine sehr große Stadt?
Ist das igh-ne sehr GRO-sse Shtatt?

Is there another available bathroom?
Gibt es noch ein Badezimmer?
Gibt es nokh ighn BAH-de-tsim-mer?

How was your trip?
Wie war deine Reise?
Vee vahr DIGH-ne RIGH-se?

Is the bathroom free?
Ist das Badezimmer frei?
Ist das BAH-de-tsim-mer frigh?

How are you feeling?
Wie geht es dir?
Vee gayt es deer?

Do you have any recommendations?
Haben Sie irgendwelche Ratschläge für mich?
HAH-ben See EER-gend-VEL-khe RAHT-shlae-ge fuer mikh?

When did you first come to China?
Wann sind Sie das erste Mal nach China gekommen?
Vann sind See das ERS-te Mahl nakh KHEE-na ge-KOM-men?

Were you born here?
Sind Sie hier geboren?
Sind See heer ge-BOH-ren?

Come join me for the rest of the vacation.
Bleibe doch für den Rest der Ferien bei mir.
BLIGH-be dokh fuer den Rest der FAYR-ee-en bigh meer.

What times do the shops open in this area?
Wann öffnen hier die Geschäfte?
Vann OEFF-nen heer dee Ge-SHAEF-te?

Is there tax-free shopping available?
Kann man dort zollfrei einkaufen?
Kann man dort TSOLL-frigh IGHN-kau-fen?

Where can I change currency?
Wo kann ich Geld wechseln?
Voh kann ikh Geld VEKH-seln?

Is it legal to drink in this area?
Darf man hier trinken?
Darf man heer TRIN-ken?

Can I smoke in this area?
Darf man hier rauchen?
Darf man heer RAU-khen?

What about this?
Wie wäre es damit?
Vee VAE-re es DAH-mit?

Can I park here?
Darf man hier parken?
Darf man heer PAR-ken?

Have you gotten used to living in Spain by now?
Haben Sie sich schon an das Leben in Spanien gewöhnt?
HAH-ben See sikh shohn an das LAY-ben in SHPAH-ni-en ge-VOEHNT?

How much does it cost to park here?
Was kostet es, hier zu parken?
Vas KOS-tet es, heer tsoo PAR-ken?

How long can I park here?
Wie lange kann ich hier parken?
Vee LAN-ge kann ikh heer PAR-ken?

Where can I get some directions?
Wo finde ich einige Hinweise?
Voh FIN-de ikh IGH-ni-ge HIN-vigh-se?

Can you point me in the direction of the bridge?
Können Sie mir den Weg zur Brücke erklären?
KOEN-nen See meer den Vayg tsoor BRUE-ke er-KLAE-ren?

What can I do here for fun?
Was kann man hier erleben?
Vas kann man heer er-LAY-ben?

Is this a family-friendly place?
Ist dieser Ort familienfreundlich?
Ist DEE-ser Ort fam-EE-lee-en-FROYND-likh?

Are kids allowed here?
Sind Kinder hier erlaubt?
Sind KIN-der heer er-LAUBT?

Where can I find the park?
Wo finde ich den Park?
Wo FIN-de ikh den Park?

How do I get back to my hotel?
Wie finde ich zurück zu meinem Hotel?
Vee FIN-de eech tsoo-RUEK tsoo MIGH-nem Ho-TEL?

Where can I get some medicine?
Wo kann ich Medikamente bekommen?
Voh kann ikh Me-dee-ka-MEN-te be-KOMM-men?

Is my passport safe here?
Ist mein Pass hier sicher?
Ist mighn Pass heer SI-kher?

Do you have a safe for my passport and belongings?
Haben Sie einen Safe für meinen Pass und meine Sachen?
HAH-ben See IGH-nen Sayf fuer MIGH-nen Pass oond MIGH-ne SA-khen?

Is it safe to be here past midnight?
Ist es hier nach Mitternacht noch sicher?
Ist es heer nakh MIT-ter-nakht nokh SI-kher?

When is the best time to visit this shop?
Wann ist die beste Zeit, um dieses Geschäft zu besuchen?
Vann ist dee BES-te Tsight, um DEE-ses Ge-SHAEFT tsoo be-SOO-khen?

What is the best hotel in the area?
Was ist das beste Hotel in der Gegend?
Vas ihst das BES-te Ho-TEL in der GAY-gend?

What attractions are close to my hotel?
Welche Attraktionen gibt es in der Nähe meines Hotels?
VEL-khe At-rak-tsee-OH-nen geebt es in der NAE-he MIGH-nes Ho-TELS?

Do you have any advice for tourists?
Haben Sie irgendwelche Tipps für Touristen?
HAH-ben See IR-gend-VEL-khe Tipps fuer Tour-IS-ten?

Do you have a list of the top things to do in the area?
Haben Sie eine Liste mit den interessantesten Aktivitäten in der Gegend?
HAH-ben See IGH-ne LIS-te mit den in-te-ress-AN-tes-ten Ak-tee-vee-TAE-ten in der GAY-gend?

What do I need to pack to go there?
Was sollte ich dorthin mitnehmen?
Vas SOLL-te ikh DORT-hin MIT-nay-men?

Can you recommend me some good food to eat?
Können Sie mir gutes Essen empfehlen?
KOEN-nen See meer GOO-tes ESS-en emp-FAY-len?

What should I do with my time here?
Was sollte ich hier unternehmen?
Vas SOLL-te ikh heer un-ter-NAY-men?

What is the cheapest way to get from my hotel to the shop?
Wie komme ich am günstigsten vom Hotel zu dem Geschäft?
Vee KOM-me ikh am GUEN-stig-sten fom Ho-TELL tsoo dem Ge-SHAEFT?

What do you think of my itinerary?
Was denken Sie über meine Route?
Vas DEN-ken See UE-ber MIGH-ne ROO-te?

Does my phone work in this country?
Funktioniert mein Telefon in diesem Land?
Funk-tsee-o-NEERT mighn TE-le-fon in DEE-sem Land?

What is the best route to get to my hotel?
Was ist die beste Route zu meinem Hotel?
Vas ist dee BES-te ROO-te tsoo MIGH-nem Ho-TELL?

Will the weather be okay for outside activities?
Ist das Wetter gut genug zum Draußensein?
Ist das VE-tter goot ge-NOOG tsum DRAU-ssen-sighn?

Was that rude?
War das unhöflich?
Vahr das OON-hoef-likh?

Where should I stay away from?
Wovon sollte ich mich fernhalten?
VOH-fon SOLL-te ikh mikh FERN-hal-ten?

What is the best dive site in the area?
Wo kann man hier gut tauchen?
Voh kann man heer goot TAU-khen?

What is the best beach in the area?
Wo ist der beste Strand in der Gegend?
Voh ist der BES-te Strahnd in der GAY-gend?

Do I need reservations?
Brauche ich eine Reservierung?
BRAU-che ikh igh-ne Re-ser-VEE-roong?

I need directions to the best local food.
Wo esse ich hier am besten?
Voh ES-se ikh heer am BES-ten?

What's your name?
Wie ist dein Name?
Vee ist dighn NAH-me?

Where is the nearest place to eat?
Wo kann man hier in der Nähe essen?
Voh kann man heer in der NAE-he ES-sen?

Where is the nearest hotel?
Wo ist das nächste Hotel?
Voh ist das NAEKH-ste Ho-TELL?

Where is transportation?
Wo gibt es Transportmöglichkeiten?
Voh geebt es Trans-PORT-moeg-likh-kigh-ten?

How much is this?
Was kostet das?
Vas KO-stet das?

Do you pay tax here?
Muss man hier Steuern zahlen?
Muss man heer STOY-ern TSAH-len?

What types of payment are accepted?
Womit kann man hier zahlen?
VOH-mit kann man heer TSAH-len?

Can you help me read this?
Können Sie mir helfen, das zu lesen?
KOEN-nen See meer HEL-fen, das tsoo LAY-sen?

What languages do you speak?
Welche Sprachen sprechen Sie?
VEL-khe SHPRAH-khen SHPRE-khen See?

Is it difficult to speak English?
Ist es schwierig, Englisch zu sprechen?
Ist es SHVEE-rig, ENG-lish tsoo SHPRE-khen?

What does that mean?
Was bedeutet das?
Vas be-DOY-tet das?

What is your name?
Wie heißen Sie?
Vee HIGH-ssen See?

Do you have a lighter?
Haben Sie ein Feuerzeug?
HAH-ben See ighn FOY-er-tsoyg?

Do you have a match?
Haben Sie ein Streichholz?
HAH-ben See ighn SHTRIGHKH-holts?

Is this a souvenir from your country?
Ist das ein Souvenir aus Ihrem Land?
Ist das ighn Soo-ve-NEER aus EE-rem Land?

What is this?
Was ist das?
Vas ist das?

Can I ask you a question?
Darf ich Ihnen eine Frage stellen?
Darf ikh EE-nen IGH-ne FRAH-ge SHTE-len?

Where is the safest place to store my travel information?
Wo bringe ich meine Reiseunterlagen am sichersten unter?
Voh BRIN-ge ikh migh-ne RIGH-se-un-ter-LAH-gen am SI-kher-sten UN-ter?

Will you come along with me?
Kommen Sie mit?
KOM-men See mit?

Is this your first time here?
Sind Sie zum ersten Mal hier?
Sind See tsum AYR-sten Mahl heer?

What is your opinion on the matter?
Was denkst du darüber?
Vas denkst doo da-RUE-ber?

Will this spoil if I leave it out too long?
Wird das schlecht, wenn ich es zu lange draußen lasse?
Vird das shlekht, venn ikh es tsoo LAN-ge DRAU-ssen LAS-se?

What side of the sidewalk do I walk on?
Auf welcher Seite des Gehsteigs soll ich gehen?
Auf VEL-kher SIGH-te des GAY-shtighgs soll ikh GAY-hen?

What do those lights mean?
Was bedeuten diese Lichter?
Vas be-DOY-ten DEE-se LIKH-ter?

Can I walk up these stairs?
Kann man diese Treppe nehmen?
Kann man DEE-se TRE-ppe NAY-men?

Is that illegal here?
Ist das verboten?
Ist das fer-BOH-ten?

How much trouble would I get in if I did that?
Bekomme ich Probleme, wenn ich das mache?
Be-KOM-me ikh Pro-BLAY-me, venn ikh das MAH-khe?

Why don't we all go together?
Warum gehen wir nicht gemeinsam?
Va-RUM GAY-hen veer nikht ge-MIGHN-sam?

May I throw away waste here?
Darf ich meinen Müll hierlassen?
Darf ikh MIGH-nen Muell HEER-las-sen?

Where is the recycle bin?
Wo ist der Mülleimer?
Voh ist der MUELL-igh-mer?

WHEN SOMEONE IS BEING RUDE

Please, close your mouth while chewing that.
Bitte halten Sie Ihren Mund geschlossen, während Sie das kauen.
BI-tte HAL-ten See EE-ren Moond ge-SHLO-ssen, WAE-rend See das KAU-en.

Don't ask me again, please.
Bitte fragen Sie mich nicht mehr.
BI-te FRAH-gen See mikh nikht mayr.

I'm not paying for that.
Dafür zahle ich nicht.
DA-fuer TSAH-le ikh nikht.

Leave me alone or I am calling the authorities.
Lassen Sie mich in Ruhe oder ich rufe die Polizei.
LA-ssen See mikh in ROO-he O-der ikh ROO-fe dee Po-lee-TSIGH.

Hurry up!
Schneller!
SHNE-ler!

Stop bothering me!
Lassen Sie mich in Ruhe!
LA-ssen See mikh in ROO-he

Don't bother me, please!
Lassen Sie mich bitte in Ruhe!
LA-ssen See mikh BI-te in ROO-he!

Are you content?
Sind Sie zufrieden?
Sind See tsoo-FREE-den?

I'm walking away, please don't follow me.
Ich gehe jetzt, bitte folgen Sie mir nicht.
Ikh GAY-he yetst, BI-te FOL-gen See meer nikht.

You stole my shoes and I would like them back.
Sie haben meine Schuhe gestohlen und ich möchte sie zurückhaben.
See HAH-ben MIGH-ne SHOO-he ge-SHTOH-len oond ikh MOEKH-te see tsoo-RUEK-hah-ben.

You have the wrong person.
Sie verwechseln mich.
See fer-WEKH-seln mikh.

I think you are incorrect.
Ich denke, das ist falsch.
IKH DEN-ke, das ist falsh.

Stop waking me up!
Hören Sie auf, mich aufzuwecken!
HOE-ren See auf, mikh AUF-tsoo-weck-en!

You're talking too much.
Sie reden zu viel.
See RAY-den tsoo feel.

That hurts!
Das tut weh!
Das toot way!

I need you to apologize.
Ich will, dass Sie sich entschuldigen.
IKH vill, dass See sikh ent-SHUL-dee-gen.

Stay away from my children!
Halten Sie sich von meinen Kindern fern!
HAL-ten See sikh fon MIGH-nen KIN-dern fern!

Don't touch me.
Berühren Sie mich nicht.
Be-RUEH-ren See mikh nikht.

I would appreciate it if you didn't take my seat.
Entschuldigung, das ist mein Platz.
Ent-SHUL-dee-goong, das ist mighn Plats.

You didn't tell me that.
Das haben Sie mir nicht gesagt.
Das HAH-ben See meer nikht ge-SAHGT.

You are price gouging me.
Das ist Wucher.
Das ist VOO-kher.

Please be quiet, I am trying to listen.
Bitte seien Sie still, ich versuche zuzuhören.
BI-te SIGH-en See shtill, ikh fer-SOO-khe TSOO-tsoo-HOE-ren.

Don't interrupt me while I am talking.
Unterbrechen Sie mich nicht.
Unter-BREKH-en See mikh nikht.

Don't sit on my car and stay away from it.
Setzen Sie sich nicht auf mein Auto und bleiben Sie weg davon.
SET-sen See sikh nikht auf mighn AU-to oond BLIGH-ben See weg da-FON.

Get out of my car.
Verlassen Sie mein Auto.
Fer-LAS-sen See mighn AU-to.

Get away from me and leave me alone!
Gehen Sie weg und lassen Sie mich in Ruhe!
GAY-hen See weg oond LAS-sen See mikh in ROO-he!

You're being rude.
Das ist unhöflich.
Das ist UN-hoef-likh.

Please don't curse around my children.
Bitte fluchen Sie nicht neben meinen Kindern.
BI-te FLOO-khen See nikht NE-ben MIGH-nen KIN-dern.

Let go of me!
Lassen Sie mich los!
LAS-sen See mikh lohs!

I'm not going to tell you again.
Ich sage das nicht noch einmal.
Ikh sah-ge das nikht nokh IGHN-mal.

Don't yell at me.
Schreien Sie mich nicht an.
SHRIGH-en See mikh nikht an.

Please lower your voice.
Bitte sprechen Sie leiser.
BI-te SHPRAY-khen See LIGH-ser.

What is the problem?
Was ist das Problem?
Vas ist das Pro-BLAYM?

I would appreciate if you didn't take pictures of me.
Bitte machen Sie keine Fotos von mir.
BI-te MA-khen See KIGH-ne FOH-tos fon meer.

I am very disappointed in the way you are behaving.
Ich bin von Ihrem Benehmen enttäuscht.
Ikh bin fon EE-rem Be-NAY-men ent-TOYSHT.

Watch where you are walking!
Passen Sie doch auf, wo Sie hinlaufen!
PA-ssen See dokh auf, wo See HIN-lau-fen!

He just bumped into me!
Er ist mir gerade reingelaufen!
Ayr ist meer ge-RAH-de RIGHN-ge-lau-fen!

MEDICAL

I would like to set up an appointment with my doctor.
Ich würde gerne einen Termin mit meinem Arzt machen.
Ikh WUER-de GER-ne IGH-nen Ter-MEEN mit MIGH-nem Artst MA-khen.

I am a new patient and need to fill out forms.
Ich bin ein neuer Patient und muss Formulare ausfüllen.
Ikh bin ighn NOY-er Pa-tsee-ENT oond muss Form-oo-LAH-re AUS-fuel-len.

I am allergic to certain medications.
Ich bin auf manche Medikamente allergisch.
Ikh bin auf MAN-khe Me-dee-ka-MEN-te a-LER-gish.

That is where it hurts.
Hier tut es weh.
Heer toot es vay.

I have had the flu for three weeks.
Ich hatte drei Wochen lang die Grippe.
Ikh HA-te drigh WO-khen lang dee GRIP-pe.

It hurts when I walk on that foot.
Es tut weh, wenn ich mit diesem Fuß auftrete.
Es toot vay, wenn ikh mit DEE-sem Fooss AUF-tre-te.

When is my next appointment?
Wann ist mein nächster Termin?
Vann ist mighn NAEKH-ster Ter-MEEN?

Does my insurance cover this?
Bezahlt das meine Versicherung?
Be-TSAHLT das migh-ne Fer-SIKH-er-oong?

Do you want to take a look at my throat?
Wollen Sie sich meinen Rachen ansehen?
VO-llen See sikh MIGH-nen RA-khen AN-se-hen?

Do I need to fast before going there?
Muss ich vorher fasten?
Muss ikh FOR-her FAS-ten?

Is there a generic version of this medicine?
Gibt es dazu auch ein Generikum?
Geebt es DA-tsoo aukh ighn Ge-NAYR-ee-kum?

I need to get back on dialysis.
Ich brauche wieder eine Dialyse.
Ikh BRAU-khe VEE-der IGH-ne Dee-a-LUE-se.

My blood type is A.
Meine Blutgruppe ist A.
MIGH-ne BLOOT-gruppe ist A.

I will be more than happy to donate blood.
Ich spende gerne Blut.
Ikh SHPEN-de GER-ne Bloot.

I have been feeling dizzy.
Mir ist schwindelig.
Meer ist SHWIN-de-lig.

The condition is getting worse.
Es wird schlimmer.
Es wird SHLIM-mer.

The medicine has made the condition a little better, but it is still there.
Die Medikamente haben ein wenig geholfen, aber ich fühle mich immer noch schlecht.
Dee Me-dee-ka-MEN-te HAH-ben ighn way-nig ge-HOL-fen, AH-ber ikh FUEH-le mikh IM-mer nokh shlekht.

Is my initial health examination tomorrow?
Ist meine erste Untersuchung morgen?
Ist MIGH-ne ERS-te Un-ter-SOO-khung MOR-gen?

I would like to switch doctors.
Ich möchte gerne zu einem anderen Arzt.
Ikh MOEKH-te GER-ne tsoo IGH-nem AN-der-en Artst.

Can you check my blood pressure?
Können Sie meinen Blutdruck messen?
KOEN-nen See MIGH-nen BLOOT-drukk ME-ssen?

I have a fever that won't go away.
Mein Fieber geht nicht weg.
MIghn FEE-ber gayt nikht weg.

I think my arm is broken.
Ich glaube, mein Arm ist gebrochen.
Ikh GLAU-be, mighn Arm ist ge-BROKH-en.

I think I have a concussion.
Ich glaube, ich habe eine Gehirnerschütterung.
Ikh GLAU-be, ikh HAH-be IGH-ne Ge-HIRN-er-SHUET-er-oong.

My eyes refuse to focus.
Meine Augen fokussieren nicht.
MIGH-ne AU-gen fo-ku-SEE-ren nikht.

I have double vision.
Ich sehe doppelt.
Ikh SAY-he DOP-pelt.

Is surgery the only way to fix this?
Ist eine Operation der einzige Weg?
Ist IGH-ne O-pe-ra-tsee-OHN der IGHN-tsee-ge Wayg?

Who are you referring me to?
An wen überweisen Sie mich?
An wayn ueber-WIGH-sen See mikh?

Where is the waiting room?
Wo ist das Wartezimmer?
Voh ist das VAR-te-tsim-mer?

Can I bring someone with me into the office?
Kann ich jemanden ins Büro mitbringen?
Kann ikh YAY-man-den ins Bue-ROH MIT-bring-en?

I need help filling out these forms.
Ich brauche Hilfe beim Ausfüllen der Formulare.
Ikh BRAU-khe HIL-fe bighm AUS-fuel-len der For-moo-LAH-re.

Do you take Cobra as an insurance provider?
Nehmen Sie Cobra als Versicherung an?
NAY-men See Cobra als Fer-SIKH-er-oong an?

What is my copayment?
Was zahle ich dazu?
Vas TSAH-le ikh da-TSOO?

What forms of payment do you accept?
Welche Zahlungsarten akzeptieren Sie?
VEL-khe TSAH-loongs-ar-ten ak-tsep-TEE-ren See?

Do you have a payment plan, or is it all due now?
Kann man auch in Raten zahlen?
Kann man aukh in RAH-ten TSAH-len?

My old doctor prescribed something different.
Mein alter Arzt hat etwas anderes verschrieben.
Mighn AL-ter Artst hat ET-was AN-de-res fer-SHREE-ben.

Will you take a look at my leg?
Können Sie sich mein Bein ansehen?
KOEN-nen See sikh mighn Bighn AN-se-hen?

I need to be referred to a gynecologist.
Ich muss zu einem Gynäkologen.
Ikh muss tsoo IGH-nem Gue-nae-ko-LOH-gen.

I am unhappy with the medicine you prescribed me.
Ich bin unzufrieden mit der Medizin, die Sie mir verschrieben haben.
Ikh bin UN-tsoo-FREE-den mit der Me-dee-TSEEN, dee See meer fer-SHREE-ben HAH-ben.

Do you see patients on the weekend?
Nehmen Sie auch am Wochenende Patienten an?
NAY-men See aukh am VO-khen-en-de Pa-tsee-EN-ten an?

I need a good therapist.
Ich brauche einen guten Therapeuten.
Ikh BRAU-khe IGH-nen GOO-ten Te-ra-POY-ten.

How long will it take me to rehab this injury?
Wie lange wird es dauern, bis die Verletzung ausheilt?
Vee LAN-ge wird es DAU-ern, bis dee Fer-LETS-oong AUS-highlt?

I have not gone to the bathroom in over a week.
Ich war über eine Woche nicht auf dem Klo.
Ikh war UE-ber IGH-ne VO-khe nikht auf dem Kloh.

I am constipated and feel bloated.
Ich habe eine Verstopfung und fühle mich aufgebläht.
Ikh HAH-be IGH-ne Fer-SHTOPF-oong oond FUE-le mikh AUF-ge-blaet.

It hurts when I go to the bathroom.
Es tut weh, wenn ich aufs Klo gehe.
Es toot vay, venn ikh aufs Kloh GAY-he.

I have not slept well at all since getting here.
Ich habe nicht geschlafen, seit ich hier bin.
Ikh HAH-be nikht ge-SHLAH-fen, sight ikh heer bin.

Do you have any pain killers?
Haben Sie Schmerzmittel?
HAH-ben See SHMERTS-mit-tel?

I am allergic to that medicine.
Ich bin allergisch auf dieses Medikament.
Ikh bin a-LER-gish auf DEE-ses Me-dee-ka-MENT.

How long will I be under observation?
Wie lange bleibe ich unter Beobachtung?
Vee LAN-ge BLIGH-be ikh UN-ter Be-OB-akh-toong?

I have a toothache.
Ich habe Zahnschmerzen.
Ikh HAH-be TSAHN-shmer-tsen.

Do I need to see a dentist?
Brauche ich einen Zahnarzt?
BRAU-che ikh IGH-nen TSAHN-artst?

Does my insurance cover dental?
Deckt meine Versicherung auch Zahnbehandlungen ab?
Dekt MIGH-ne Fer-SIKH-er-oong aukh TSAHN-be-HAND-loong-en ab?

My diarrhea won't go away.
Mein Durchfall wird nicht besser.
Mighn DOORKH-fall vird nikht BE-sser.

Can I have a copy of the receipt for my insurance?
Kann ich eine Kopie des Rezeptes für meine Versicherung haben?
Kann ikh IGH-ne Ko-PEE des Re-TSEP-tes fuer MIGH-ne Fer-SIKH-er-oong HAH-ben?

I need a pregnancy test.
Ich brauche einen Schwangerschaftstest.
Ikh BRAU-khe IGH-nen SHWANG-er-shafts-test.

I think I may be pregnant.
Ich glaube, ich bin schwanger.
Ikh GLAU-be, ikh bin SHWANG-er.

Can we please see a pediatrician?
Können wir einen Kinderarzt aufsuchen?
KOEN-nen veer IGH-nen KIN-der-artst AUF-soo-khen?

I have had troubles breathing.
Ich habe Probleme mit dem Atmen.
Ikh HAH-be Pro-BLAY-me mit daym AHT-men.

My sinuses are acting up.
Meine Nebenhöhlen wirken entzündet.
MIGH-ne NAY-ben-HOE-len WIR-ken ent-TSUEN-det.

Will I still be able to breastfeed?
Werde ich stillen können?
VAYR-de ikh SHTILL-en KOEN-nen?

How long do I have to stay in bed?
Wie lang muss ich im Bett bleiben?
Vee lang muss ikh im Bett BLIGH-ben?

How long do I have to stay under hospital care?
Wie lange muss ich im Krankenhaus bleiben?
Vee LAN-ge muss ikh im KRAN-ken-haus BLIGH-ben?

Is it contagious?
Ist es ansteckend?
Ist es AN-shtek-end?

How far along am I?
Wie weit ist es fortgeschritten?
Vee vight ist es FORT-ge-shrit-ten?

What did the x-ray say?
Was sagt das Röntgenbild?
Vas sahgt das ROENT-gen-bild?

Can I walk without a cane?
Kann ich ohne Stock gehen?
Kann ikh OH-ne Shtok GAY-hen?

Is the wheelchair necessary?
Brauche ich einen Rollstuhl?
BRAU-khe ikh IGH-nen ROLL-shtool?

Am I in the right area of the hospital?
Bin ich im richtigen Bereich des Krankenhauses?
Bin ikh im RIKH-tee-gen Be-RIGHKH des KRAN-ken-hau-ses?

Where is the front desk receptionist?
Wo ist die Anmeldung?
Voh ist dee AN-mel-doong?

I would like to go to a different waiting area.
Ich würde gerne woanders warten.
Ikh WUER-de GER-ne wo-AN-ders WAR-ten.

Can I have a change of sheets, please?
Kann ich bitte andere Laken haben?
Kann ikh BI-te AN-de-re LAH-ken HAH-ben?

Excuse me, what is your name?
Entschuldigen Sie, wie ist Ihr Name?
Ent-SHUL-dee-gen See, vee ist Eer NAH-me?

Who is the doctor in charge here?
Wer ist hier der verantwortliche Arzt?
Vayr ist heer dayr fer-ANT-wort-lee-khe Artst?

I need some assistance, please.
Ich brauche etwas Unterstützung bitte.
Ikh BRAU-khe ET-was Un-ter-STUE-tsoong BI-te.

Will my recovery affect my ability to do work?
Werde ich arbeiten können?
VAYR-de ikh AR-bigh-ten KOEN-nen?

How long is the estimated recovery time?
Wie lange werde ich mich erholen müssen?
Vee LAN-ge VAYR-de ikh mikh er-HO-len MUES-sen?

Is that all you can do for me? There has to be another option.
Ist das alles was Sie für mich tun können? Es muss noch andere
Optionen geben.
Ist das AL-les vas See fuer mikh toon KOEN-nen? Es muss nokh AN-de-re
Op-tsee-OH-nen GAY-ben.

I need help with motion sickness.
Ich brauche etwas für meine Reisekrankheit.
Ikh BRAU-che ET-was fuer MIGH-ne RIGH-se-krank-hight.

I'm afraid of needles.
Ich habe Angst vor Spritzen.
Ikh HAH-be Angst for SHPRI-tsen.

My gown is too small; I need another one.
Meine Kleidung ist zu eng, ich brauche eine andere.
MIGH-ne KLIGH-doong ist tsoo eng, ikh BRAU-khe IGH-ne AN-de-re.

Can I have extra pillows?
Kann ich zusätzliche Kissen haben?
Kann ikh TSOO-saets-lee-khe KI-ssen HAH-ben?

I need assistance getting to the bathroom.
Ich brauche Hilfe, um zum Klo zu kommen.
Ikh BRAU-khe HIL-fe, um tsum Kloh tsoo KOM-men.

Hi, is the doctor in?
Hallo, ist der Arzt da?
HA-lo, ist der Artst da?

When should I schedule the next checkup?
Wann sollen wir den nächsten Termin vereinbaren?
Vann SOL-len veer den NAEKH-sten Ter-MEEN fer-IGHN-bah-ren?

When can I have these stitches removed?
Wann können wir die Nähte entfernen?
Vann KOEN-nen veer dee NAE-te ent-FER-nen?

Do you have any special instructions while I'm in this condition?
Haben Sie zusätzliche Anweisungen für diese Zeit?
HAH-ben See TSOO-saets-lee-khe AN-wigh-sung-en fuer DEE-se Tsight?

ORDERING FOOD

Can I see the menu?
Kann ich eine Speisekarte haben?
Kann ikh IGH-ne SHPIGH-se-kar-te HAH-ben?

I'm really hungry. We should eat something soon.
Ich habe wirklich Hunger. Wir sollten bald etwas essen.
Ikh HAH-be VIR-klikh HOON-ger. Veer SOL-ten bald ET-was ES-sen.

Can I take a look in the kitchen?
Kann ich einen Blick in die Küche werfen?
Kann ikh IGH-nen Blikk in dee KUE-khe VER-fen?

Can we see the drink menu?
Können wir die Getränkekarte sehen?
KOEN-nen veer dee Ge-TRAEN-ke-kar-te SAY-hen?

When can we be seated?
Wann können wir uns setzen?
Vann KOEN-nen veer uns SE-tsen?

This is very tender and delicious.
Das ist sehr zart und lecker.
Das ist sayr tsahrt oond LE-kker.

Do you serve alcohol?
Haben Sie alkoholische Getränke?
HAH-ben See al-ko-HO-li-she Ge-TRAEN-ke?

I'm afraid our party can't make it.
Unsere Gruppe schafft es leider nicht.
UN-se-re GRU-pe shafft es LIGH-der nikht.

That room is reserved for us.
Dieser Raum ist für uns reserviert.
DEE-ser Raum ist fuer uns re-ser-VEERT.

Are there any seasonal favorites that you serve?
Bieten Sie saisonale Spezialitäten an?
BEE-ten See say-so-NAH-le Shpe-tsee-a-lee-TAE-ten an?

Do you offer discounts for kids or seniors?
Bieten Sie Rabatte für Kinder oder Senioren an?
BEE-ten See Ra-BA-tte fuer KIN-der OH-der Se-nee-OH-ren an?

I would like it filleted.
Ich möchte es filetiert.
Ikh MOEKH-te es feel-le-TEERT.

I would like to reserve a table for a party of four.
Ich möchte gerne einen Tisch für vier reservieren.
Ikh MOEKH-te GAYR-ne IGH-nen Tish fuer feer re-ser-VEE-ren.

I would like to place the reservation under my name.
Ich möchte die Reservierung bitte unter meinem Namen vornehmen.
Ikh MOEKH-te dee Re-ser-VEE-roong BI-te UN-ter MIGH-nem NAH-men FOR-nay-men.

What type of alcohol do you serve?
Was haben Sie an alkoholischen Getränken da?
Vas HAH-ben See an al-ko-HO-li-shen Ge-TRAEN-ken da?

Do I need a reservation?
Brauche ich eine Reservierung?
BRAU-khe ikh IGH-ne Re-ser-VEE-roong?

What does it come with?
Was gibt es an Beilagen?
Vas geebt es an BIGH-lah-gen?

What are the ingredients?
Was sind die Zutaten?
Vas sind dee TSOO-tah-ten?

What else does the chef put in the dish?
Was gibt der Koch sonst noch hinzu?
Vas geebt der Kokh sonst nokh hin-TSOO?

I wonder which of these tastes better?
Ich frage mich, welches besser schmeckt.
Ikh FRAH-ge mikh, VEL-khes BE-sser shmekkt.

That is incorrect. Our reservation was at noon.
Das ist nicht richtig. Unsere Reservierung war auf Mittag.
Das ist nikht RIKH-tig. UN-se-re Re-ser-VEE-roong vahr auf MI-tahg.

I would like red wine, please.
Ich möchte bitte Rotwein.
Ikh MOECH-te BI-te ROHT-vighn.

Can you choose the soup?
Kann man die Suppe aussuchen?
Kann man dee SU-ppe AUS-soo-khen?

What is the most popular dish here?
Was essen die Leute hier am liebsten?
Vas E-ssen dee LOY-te heer am LEEB-sten?

What are the specials today?
Welche Tagesgerichte gibt es heute?
VEL-khe TAH-ges-ge-RIKH-te geebt es HOY-te?

What are your appetizers?
Welche Vorspeisen haben Sie?
VEL-khe FOHR-shpigh-sen HAH-ben See?

Please bring these out separately.
Bitte servieren Sie diese getrennt.
BI-te ser-VEE-ren See DEE-se ge-TRENNT.

Do we leave a tip?
Geben wir Trinkgeld?
GAY-ben veer TRINK-geld?

Are tips included with the bill?
Enthält die Rechnung das Trinkgeld?
Ent-haelt dee Rech-noong das Treenk-geld?

Split the bill, please.
Teilen Sie die Rechnung bitte auf.
TIGH-len See dee REKH-noong BI-te auf.

We are paying separately.
Wir zahlen getrennt.
Veer TSAH-len ge-TRENNT.

Is there an extra fee for sharing an entrée?

Zahlen wir etwas extra, wenn wir uns ein Gericht teilen?

TSAH-len veer ET-was EKS-tra, venn veer uns ighn Ge-RIKHT TIGH-len?

Is there a local specialty that you recommend?

Können Sie eine regionale Spezialität empfehlen?

KOE-nen See IGH-ne re-gee-o-NAH-le Shpay-tsee-a-lee-TAET em-PFAE-len?

This looks different from what I originally ordered.

Das sieht anders aus als das, was ich bestellt habe.

Das seet AN-ders aus als das vas ikh be-SHTELLT HAH-be.

Is this a self-serve buffet?

Ist hier Selbstbedienung?

Ist heer SELBST-be-dee-noong?

I want a different waiter.

Ich möchte eine andere Bedienung.

Ikh MOECH-te IGH-ne AN-de-re Be-DEE-noong.

Please move us to a different table.

Können wir einen anderen Tisch haben?

KOE-nen veer IGH-nen AN-der-en Tish HAH-ben?

Can we put two tables together?

Können wir zwei Tische zusammenstellen?

KOE-nen veer tsvigh TI-she tsoo-SAH-men-shtel-len?

My spoon is dirty. Can I have another one?

Mein Löffel ist schmutzig. Kann ich einen anderen haben?

Mighn LOE-fel ist SHMOO-tsig. Kann ikh IGH-nen AN-de-ren HAH-ben?

We need more napkins, please.

Wir brauchen mehr Servietten, bitte.

Veer BRAU-khen mayr Ser-vee-ET-ten, BI-te.

I'm a vegetarian and don't eat meat.

Male: Ich bin Vegetarier und esse kein Fleisch.

Ikh bin Ve-ge-TAH-ree-er oond E-sse kighn Flighsh.

Female: Ich bin Vegetarierin und esse kein Fleisch.

Ikh bin Ve-ge-TAH-ree-er–in oond E-sse kighn Flighsh.

The table next to us is being too loud. Can you say something?
Der Tisch neben uns ist zu laut. Können Sie etwas sagen?
Der Tish NAY-ben uns ist tsoo laut. KOE-nen See ET-vas SAH-gen?

Someone is smoking in our non-smoking section.
Jemand raucht im Nichtraucherbereich.
YAY-mand raukht im NIKHT-rau-kher-be-RIGHKH.

Please seat us in a booth.
Bitte teilen Sie uns eine Sitzecke zu.
BI-te TIGH-len See uns IGH-ne SITS-ekke tsoo.

Do you have any non-alcoholic beverages?
Haben Sie auch etwas ohne Alkohol?
HAH-ben See aukh ET-vas OH-ne AL-ko-hol?

Where is your bathroom?
Wo ist das Klo?
Voh ist das Kloh?

Are you ready to order?
Sind Sie bereit, zu bestellen?
Sind See be-RIGHT, tsoo be-SHTE-len?

Five more minutes, please.
Noch fünf Minuten bitte.
Nokh fuenf Mee-NOO-ten BI-te.

What time do you close?
Wann schließen Sie?
Vann SHLEE-ssen See?

Is there pork in this dish? I don't eat pork.
Enthält das Schweinefleisch? Ich esse kein Schweinefleisch.
Ent-HALET das SHVIGH-ne-flighsh? Ikh E-sse kighn SHVIGH-ne-flighsh.

Do you have any dishes for vegans?
Haben Sie etwas für Veganer?
HAH-ben See ET-vas fuer Ve-gAH-ner?

Are these vegetables fresh?
Ist dieses Gemüse frisch?
Ist DEE-ses Ge-MUE-se frish?

Have any of these vegetables been cooked in butter?
Wurde dieses Gemüse in Butter gekocht?
VOOR-de DEE-ses Ge-MUE-se in BU-ter ge-KOKHT?

Is this spicy?
Ist das scharf?
Ist das sharf?

Is this sweet?
Ist das süß?
Ist das suess?

I want more, please.
Mehr davon, bitte.
Mayr da-FON, BI-te.

I would like a dish containing these items.
Ich möchte gern ein Gericht mit diesen Zutaten bestellen.
Ikh MOEKH-te gayrn ighn Ge-RIKHT mit DEE-sen TSOO-tah-ten be-SHTEL-len.

Can you make this dish light? Thank you.
Können Sie dieses Gericht kalorienarm zubereiten? Danke.
KOE-nen See DEE-ses Ge-RIKHT ka-lo-REEN-arm TSOO-be-righ-ten? DAN-ke.

Nothing else.
Nichts weiter.
Nikhts VIGH-ter.

Please clear the plates.
Bitte räumen Sie ab.
BI-te ROY-men See ab.

May I have a cup of soup?
Kann ich die Suppe haben?
Kann ikh dee SU-pe HAH-ben?

Do you have any bar snacks?
Haben Sie Snacks?
HAH-ben See Snaeks?

Another round, please.
Mehr davon, bitte.
Mayr da-FON, BI-te.

When is closing time for the bar?
Wann schließt die Bar?
Vann shleest dee Bahr?

That was delicious!
Das war lecker!
Das vahr LE-kker!

Does this have alcohol in it?
Enthält das Alkohol?
Ent-HAELT das AL-ko-hol?

Does this have nuts in it?
Enthält das Nüsse?
Ent-HAELT das NUE-sse?

Is this gluten free?
Ist das glutenfrei?
Ist das gloo-TAYN-frigh?

Can I get this to go?
Kann ich das zum Mitnehmen haben?
Kann ikh das tsum MIT-nay-men HAH-ben?

May I have a refill?
Kann ich noch mehr haben?
Kann ikh nokh mayr HAH-ben?

Is this dish kosher?
Ist dieses Gericht koscher?
ist DEE-ses Ge-rikht KOH-sher?

I would like to change my drink.
Ich möchte gerne etwas anderes trinken.
Ikh MOEKH-te GAYR-ne ET-vas AN-de-res TRIN-ken.

My coffee is cold. Could you please warm it up?
Mein Kaffee ist kalt. Können Sie ihn bitte aufwärmen?
Mighn KA-fay ist kalt. KOE-nen See een BI-te AUF-waer-men?

Do you serve coffee?
Haben Sie Kaffee?
HAH-ben See KA-fay?

Can I please have cream in my coffee?
Kann ich Milch in meinen Kaffee haben?
Kann ikh Milkh in MIGH-nen KA-fay HAH-ben?

Please add extra sugar to my coffee.
Bitte geben Sie mehr Zucker in meinen Kaffee.
BI-te GAY-ben See mayr TSU-kker in MIGH-nen KA-fay.

I would like to have my coffee served black, no cream and no sugar.
Einen schwarzen Kaffee bitte, ohne Milch und Zucker.
IGH-nen SHVAR-tsen KA-fay BI-te, OH-ne Milkh oond TSU-kker.

I would like to have decaffeinated coffee, please.
Einen koffeinfreien Kaffee, bitte.
IGH-nen ko-fe-EEN-frigh-en KA-fay, BI-te.

Do you serve coffee-flavored ice cream?
Haben Sie Kaffee-Eis?
HAH-ben See KA-fay-ighs?

Please put my cream and sugar on the side so that I can add it myself.
Bitte Milch und Zucker extra zum Selbsteinfüllen.
BI-te Milkh oond TSU-kker EKS-tra tsum SELBST-ighn-fuel-len.

I would like to order an iced coffee.
Einen Eiskaffee, bitte.
IGH-nen IGHS-kaf-fay, BI-te.

I would like an espresso please.
Einen Espresso, bitte.
IGH-nen Es-PRE-sso, BI-te.

Do you have 2% milk?
Haben Sie fettarme Milch?
HAH-ben See FETT-ar-me Milkh?

Do you serve soy milk?
Haben Sie Sojamilch?
HAH-ben See SOH-ya-milkh?

Do you have almond milk?
Haben Sie Mandelmilch?
HAH-ben See MAN-del-milkh?

Are there any alternatives to the milk you serve?
Haben Sie Alternativen zur Milch?
HAH-ben See Al-ter-na-TEE-fen tsoor Milkh?

Please put the lemons for my tea on the side.
Bitte servieren Sie die Zitronen für den Tee extra.
BI-te ser-VEE-ren See dee Tsee-TROH-nen fuer den Tay EKS-tra.

No lemons with my tea, thank you.
Keine Zitronen für den Tee, danke.
KIGH-ne Tsee-TROH-nen fuer den Tay, DAN-ke.

Is your water from the tap?
Ist das Leitungswasser?
Ist das LIGH-tungs-vas-ser?

Sparkling water, please.
Mineralwasser, bitte.
Mee-ner-AHL-vas-ser, BI-te.

Can I get a diet coke?
Kann ich eine Diät-Cola haben?
Kann ikh IGH-ne Dee-AET-Ko-la HAH-ben?

We're ready to order.
Wir sind bereit, zu bestellen.
Veer sind be-RIGHT tsoo be-SHTEL-len.

Can we be seated over there instead?
Können wir auch dort drüben sitzen?
KOE-nen veer aukh dort DRUE-ben SI-tsen?

Can we have a seat outside?
Können wir draußen sitzen?
KOE-nen veer DRAU-ssen SI-tsen?

Please hold the salt.
Bitte sparen Sie mit dem Salz.
BI-te SHPAH-ren See mit dem Salts.

This is what I would like for my main course.
Das möchte ich als Hauptgericht.
Das MOEKH-te ich als HAUPT-ge-rikht.

I would like the soup instead of the salad.
Ich möchte gerne die Suppe statt des Salats.
Ich MOEKH-te GAYR-ne dee SU-pe shtatt des Sa-LAHTS.

I'll have the chicken risotto.
Ich möchte gerne das Hühner-Risotto.
Ikh MOEKH-te GAYR-ne das HUE-ner-Ree-SO-tto.

Can I change my order?
Kann ich meine Bestellung ändern?
Kann ikh MIGH-ne Be-SHTEL-loong AEN-dern?

Do you have a kids' menu?
Haben Sie eine Speisekarte für Kinder?
HAH-ben See IGH-ne SHPIGH-se-kar-te fuer KIN-der?

When does the lunch menu end?
Bis wann gibt es die Mittagskarte?
Bis vann geebt es die MI-tahgs-kar-te?

When does the dinner menu start?
Ab wann gibt es die Abendkarte?
Ab vann geebt es dee AH-bend-kar-te?

Do you have any recommendations from the menu?
Haben Sie irgendwelche Empfehlungen?
HAH-ben See IR-gend-wel-khe Em-PFAE-loong-en?

I would like to place an off-menu order.
Ich möchte gerne etwas bestellen, was nicht auf der Speisekarte ist.
Ikh MOEKH-te GAYR-ne ET-was be-SHTEL-len, vas nikht auf der SHPIGH-se-kar-te ist.

Can we see the dessert menu?
Können wir die Dessertkarte haben?
KOE-nen veer dee Des-SAYR-kar-te HAH-ben?

Is this available sugar-free?
Gibt's das auch zuckerfrei?
Geebts das aukh TSU-kker-frigh?

May we have the bill, please?
Die Rechnung, bitte.
Dee REKH-noong, BI-te.

Where do we pay?
Wo zahlen wir?
Voh TSAH-len veer?

Hi, we are with the party of Isaac.
Hallo, wir gehören zu Isaac.
HA-lo, veer ge-HOE-ren tsoo Isaac.

We haven't made up our minds yet on what to order. Can we have a few more minutes, please?
Wir brauchen noch etwas.
Veer BRAU-khen nokh ET-was.

Waiter!
Kellner!
KELL-ner!

Waitress!
Kellnerin!
KELL-ner-in!

I'm still deciding, come back to me, please.
Ich bin noch nicht soweit, bitte kommen Sie später wieder.
Ikh bin nokh nikht so-VIGHT, BI-te KOM-men See SHPAE-ter VEE-der.

Can we have a pitcher of that?
Können wir einen Krug davon haben?
KOE-nen veer IGH-nen Kroog da-FON HAH-ben?

This is someone else's meal.
Das hat jemand anderes bestellt.
Das hat YAY-mand AN-der-es be-SHTELLT.

Can you please heat this up a little more?
Können Sie das ein wenig mehr aufwärmen?
KOE-nen See das ighn VAY-nig mayr AUF-vaer-men?

I'm afraid I didn't order this.
Das habe ich nicht bestellt.
Das HAH-be ikh nikht be-SHTELLT.

The same thing again, please.
Das Gleiche noch einmal bitte.
Das GLIGH-khe noch IGHN-mal BI-te.

Can we have another bottle of wine?
Können wir noch eine Flasche Wein haben?
KOE-nen veer nokh IGH-ne FLA-she Vighn HAH-ben?

That was perfect, thank you!
Das war perfekt, danke!
Das vahr per-FEKT, DAN-ke!

Everything was good.
Alles war gut.
AL-les vahr goot.

Can we have the bill?
Die Rechnung, bitte.
Dee REKH-noong, BI-te.

I'm sorry, but this bill is incorrect.
Entschuldigen Sie, die Rechnung stimmt nicht.
Ent-SHUL-dee-gen See, dee REKH-noong shtimmt nikht.

Can I have clean cutlery?
Kann ich sauberes Besteck haben?
Kann ikh SAU-ber-es Be-SHTEKK HAH-ben?

Can we have more napkins?
Können wir mehr Servietten haben?
KOE-nen veer mayr Ser-vee-ET-ten HAH-ben?

May I have another straw?
Kann ich noch einen Strohhalm haben?
Kann ikh nokh IGH-nen SHTROH-halm HAH-ben?

What sides can I have with that?
Welche Beilagen kann ich dazu haben?
VEL-khe BIGH-lah-gen kann ikh da-TSOO HAH-ben?

Excuse me, but this is overcooked.
Entschuldigen Sie, aber das ist verbrannt.
Ent-SHUL-dee-gen See, AH-ber das ist fer-BRANNT.

May I talk to the chef?
Kann ich den Koch sprechen?
Kann ikh den KOKH SHPREKH-en?

We have booked a table for fifteen people.
Wir haben einen Tisch für fünfzehn Personen reserviert.
Veer HAH-ben IGH-nen Tish fuer FUENF-tsaehn Per-SOH-nen re-ser-VEERT.

Are there any tables free?
Sind noch Tische frei?
Sind nokh TI-she frigh?

I would like one beer, please.
Ein Bier, bitte.
Ighn Beer, BI-te.

Can you add ice to this?
Kann ich dazu Eis haben?
Kann ikh DAH-tsoo Ighs HAH-ben?

I would like to order a dark beer.
Ein Schwarzbier, bitte.
Ighn SHVARTS-beer, BI-te.

Do you have any beer from the tap?
Haben Sie Zapfbier?
HAH-ben See TSAPF-beer?

How expensive is your champagne?
Was kostet der Champagner?
Vas KOS-tet der Sham-PAN-yer?

Enjoy your meal.
Guten Appetit!
GOO-ten Ap-pe-TEET!

I want this.
Das bitte.
DAS BI-te.

Please cook my meat well done.
Bitte machen Sie es well done.
BI-te MA-khen See es well done.

Please cook my meat medium rare.
Bitte machen Sie es medium rare.
BI-te MA-khen See es medium rare.

Please prepare my meat rare.
Bitte machen Sie es rare.
BI-te MA-khen See es rare.

What type of fish do you serve?
Was haben Sie an Fisch da?
Vas HAH-ben See an Fish da?

Can I make a substitution with my meal?
Kann ich etwas umbestellen?
Kann ikh ET-was UM-be-shtel-len?

Do you have a booster seat for my child?
Haben Sie eine Sitzerhöhung für mein Kind?
HAH-ben See IGH-ne SITS-er-HOE-oong fuer mighn Kind?

Call us when you get a table.
Rufen Sie uns, wenn ein Tisch frei wird.
ROOF-en See uns, venn ighn Tish frigh vird.

Is this a non-smoking section?
Ist das ein Nichtraucherbereich?
Ist das ighn NIKHT-rau-kher-be-righkh?

We would like to be seated in the smoking section.
Wir möchten gerne im Raucherbereich sitzen.
Veer MOEKH-ten GAYR-ne im RAU-kher-be-righkh SI-tsen.

This meat tastes funny.
Das Fleisch schmeckt seltsam.
Das Flighsh shmekt SELT-sam.

More people will be joining us later.
Einige von uns kommen später noch nach.
IGH-ni-ge fon oons KOM-men SHPAE-ter nokh nahkh.

TRANSPORTATION

Where's the train station?
Wo ist der Bahnhof?
Voh ist der BAHN-hof?

How much does it cost to get to this address?
Was kostet es, zu dieser Adresse zu gelangen?
Vas KOS-tet es, tsoo DEE-ser A-DRES-se tsoo ge-LANG-en?

What type of payment do you accept?
Welche Zahlungsmöglichkeiten gibt es?
VEL-khe TSAH-loongs-moeg-likh-kigh-ten geebt es?

Do you have first-class tickets available?
Gibt es Erste-Klasse-Tickets?
Geebt es ERS-te-KLAS-se-Tik-kets?

What platform do I need to be on to catch this train?
Auf welchem Bahnsteig fährt der Zug ein?
Auf VEL-khem BAHN-shtighg faert der Tsoog ighn?

Are the roads paved in this area?
Gibt es dort gute Straßen?
Geebt es dort GOO-te SHTRAH-ssen?

Where are the dirt roads, and how do I avoid them?
Wo sind unbefestigte Straßen und wie vermeide ich sie?
Voh sind UN-be-fes-tig-te STRAH-ssen oond vee fer-MIGH-de ikh see?

Are there any potholes I need to avoid?
Gibt es Schlaglöcher?
Geebt es SHLAHG-loe-kher?

How fast are you going?
Wie schnell fährst du?
Vee shnell faerst doo?

Do I need to put my emergency blinkers on?
Soll ich meine Warnblinker einschalten?
Soll ikh MIGH-ne VARN-blink-er IGHN-shal-ten?

Make sure to use the right turn signals.
Achten Sie darauf, den richtigen Blinker zu verwenden.
AKH-ten See da-RAUF, den RIKH-tee-gen BLIN-ker tsoo fer-VEN-den.

We need a good mechanic.
Wir brauchen einen guten Mechaniker.
Veer BRAU-khen IGH-nen GOO-ten Me-KHA-nee-ker.

Can we get a push?
Kann uns jemand Starthilfe geben?
Kann uns YAY-mand SHTAHRT-hil-fe GAY-ben?

I have to call the towing company to move my car.
Ich muss den Abschleppdienst rufen.
Ikh muss den AB-shlepp-deenst ROO-fen.

Make sure to check the battery and spark plugs for any problems.
Überprüfen Sie bei Problemen die Batterie und die Anschlüsse.
UE-ber-PRUE-fen See bigh Pro-BLAY-men dee Ba-ter-EE oond dee AN-shlue-sse.

Check the oil level.
Prüfe den Ölstand.
PRUE-fe den OEL-shtand.

I need to notify my insurance company.
Ich muss meiner Versicherung Bescheid geben.
Ikh muss MIGH-ner Fer-SIKH-er-oong Be-SHIGHD GAY-ben.

When do I pay the taxi driver?
Wann bezahle ich den Taxifahrer?
Vann be-TSAH-le ikh den TAK-see-fah-rer?

Please take me to the nearest train station.
Bitte bringen Sie mich zum nächsten Bahnhof.
BI-te BRIN-gen See mikh tsum NAEKH-sten BAHN-hof.

How long does it take to get to this address?
Wie lange brauchen wir bis zu dieser Adresse?
Vee LAN-ge BRAU-khen veer bis tsoo DEE-ser A-DRES-se?

Can you stop here, please?
Können Sie bitte hier anhalten?
KOE-nen See BI-te heer AN-hal-ten?

You can drop me off anywhere around here.
Sie können mich hier irgendwo absetzen.
See KOE-nen mikh heer IR-gend-vo AB-set-sen.

Is there a charge for extra passengers?
Kosten zusätzliche Passagiere extra?
KOS-ten TSOO-saets-likh-e Pas-sa-SHEE-re EKS-tra?

What is the condition of the road? Is it safe to travel there?
Wie sind die Straßen dort? Sind sie sicher genug?
Vee sind dee SHTRAH-ssen dort? Sind see SI-kher ge-NOOG?

Take me to the emergency room.
Bringen Sie mich in die Notaufnahme.
BRIN-gen See mikh in dee NOHT-auf-nah-me.

Take me to the embassy.
Bringen Sie mich zur Botschaft.
BRIN-gen See mikh tsoor BOT-shaft.

I want to travel around the country.
Ich möchte im Land herumreisen.
Ikh MOEKH-te im Land her-UM-righ-sen.

Is this the right side of the road?
Ist das die richtige Straßenseite?
Ist das dee RIKH-tee-ge SHTRAH-ssen-sigh-te?

My car broke down, please help!
Mein Auto ist kaputt, bitte helfen Sie mir!
Mighn AU-to ist ka-PUTT, BI-te HEL-fen See meer!

Can you help me change my tire?
Können Sie mir helfen, meinen Reifen zu wechseln?
KOE-nen See meer HEL-fen, MIGH-nen RIGH-fen tsoo WEKH-seln?

Where can I get a rental car?
Wo kann ich ein Auto mieten?
Voh kann ikh ighn AU-to MEE-ten?

Please take us to the hospital.
Bitte bringen Sie uns zum Krankenhaus.
BI-te BRIN-gen See uns tsoom KRAN-ken-haus.

Is that the car rental office?
Ist das der Autoverleih?
Ist das der AU-to-fer-ligh?

May I have a price list for your fleet?
Kann ich eine Preisliste für die Flotte haben?
Kann ikh IGH-ne PRIGHS-lis-te fuer dee FLO-te HAH-ben?

Can I get insurance on this rental car?
Kann ich diesen Mietwagen versichern lassen?
Kann ikh DEE-sen MEET-vah-gen fer-SIKH-ern LA-ssen?

How much is the car per day?
Was kostet das Auto am Tag?
Vas KOS-tet das AU-to am Tahg?

How many kilometers can I travel with this car?
Wie viele Kilometer kann ich mit diesem Auto fahren?
Vee FEE-le Kee-lo-MAY-ter kann ikh meet DEE-sem AU-to FAH-ren?

I would like maps of the region if you have them.
Ich bräuchte eine Karte der Region, falls Sie eine haben.
Ikh BOYKH-te IGH-ne KAR-te der Re-gee-OHN, falls See IGH-ne HAH-ben.

When I am done with the car, where do I return it?
Wohin bringe ich das Auto danach zurück?
Voh-HIN BRIN-ge ikh das AU-to da-NAKH tsoo-RUEK?

Is this a standard or automatic transmission?
Ist das ein Schalt- oder ein Automatikgetriebe?
Ist das ighn Shalt- oh-der ighn Au-to-MAH-tik-ge-TREE-be?

Is this car gas-efficient? How many kilometers per liter?
Welchen Verbrauch hat das Auto?
VEL-chen Fer-BRAUCH hat das AU-to?

Where is the spare tire stored?
Wo ist der Ersatzreifen?
Voh ist der Er-SATS-righ-fen?

Are there places around the city that are difficult to drive?
Gibt es hier Orte, die schwer befahrbar sind?
Geebt es heer OR-te, dee shwayr be-FAHR-bar sind?

At what time of the day is the traffic the worst?
Wann am Tag ist der Verkehr am schlimmsten?
Vann am Tahg ist der Ver-kayr am SHLIMM-sten?

We can't park right here.
Wir können hier nicht parken.
Veer KOE-nen heer nikht PAR-ken.

What is the speed limit?
Wie schnell darf man hier fahren?
Vee shnell darf man heer FAH-ren?

Keep the change.
Behalten Sie das Restgeld.
Be-HAL-ten See das REST-geld.

Now let's get off here.
Jetzt lass uns verschwinden.
Yetst lass uns fer-SHVIN-den.

Where is the train station?
Wo ist der Bahnhof?
Voh ist der BAHN-hof?

Is the bus stop nearby?
Ist die Bushaltestelle in der Nähe?
Ist dee BUS-hal-te-shtel-le in der NAE-he?

When does the bus run?
Wann kommt der Bus?
Vann kommt der Bus?

Where do I go to catch a taxi?
Wo finde ich ein Taxi?
Voh FIN-de ikh ighn TAK-see?

Does the train go to the north station?
Fährt der Zug zum Nordbahnhof?
Faert der Tsoog tsum NORD-bahn-hof?

Where do I go to purchase tickets?
Wo kann ich Fahrkarten kaufen?
Voh kann ikh FAHR-kar-ten KAU-fen?

How much is a ticket to the north?
Wie viel kostet eine Fahrkarte in den Norden?
Vee FEEL KOS-tet IGH-ne FAHR-kar-te in den NOR-den?

What is the next stop along this route?
Was ist der nächste Halt entlang dieser Route?
Vas ist der NAEKH-ste Halt ent-LANG DEE-ser ROO-te?

Can I have a ticket to the north?
Kann ich eine Fahrkarte in den Norden haben?
Kann ikh IGH-ne FAHR-kar-te in den NOR-den HAH-ben?

Where is my designated platform?
Wo ist mein Bahnsteig?
Voh ist mighn BAHN-stighg?

Where do I place my luggage?
Wo stelle ich mein Gepäck ab?
Voh SHTEL-le ikh mighn Ge-PAEK ab?

Are there any planned closures today?
Gibt es heute Verkehrsbehinderungen?
Geebt es HOY-te Fer-KAYRS-be-HIN-de-roong-en?

Where are the machines that disperse tickets?
Wo sind die Fahrkartenautomaten?
Voh sind dee FAHR-kar-ten-au-to-MAH-ten?

Does this car come with insurance?
Ist dieses Auto versichert?
Ist DEE-ses AU-to fer-SIKH-ert?

May I have a timetable, please?
Kann ich einen Fahrplan haben?
Kann ikh IGH-nen FAHR-plan HAH-ben?

How often do trains come to this area?
Wie oft hält hier ein Zug?
Vee oft haelt heer ighn Tsoog?

Is the train running late?
Ist der Zug verspätet?
Ist der Tsoog fer-SHPAE-tet?

Has the train been cancelled?
Kommt der Zug noch?
Kommt der Tsoog nokh?

Is this seat available?
Ist dieser Platz noch frei?
Ist DEE-ser Plats nokh frigh?

Do you mind if I sit here?
Darf ich hier sitzen?
Darf ikh heer SI-tsen?

I've lost my ticket.
Ich habe meine Fahrkarte verloren.
Ikh HAH-be MIGH-ne FAHR-kar-te fer-LOH-ren.

Excuse me, this is my stop.
Entschuldigen Sie, das ist meine Haltestelle.
Ent-SHOOL-dee-gen See, das ist MIGH-ne HAL-te-shtel-le.

Can you please open the window?
Können Sie bitte das Fenster öffnen?
KOE-nen See BI-te das FEN-ster OEFF-nen?

Is smoking allowed in the car?
Ist Rauchen im Waggon erlaubt?
Ist RAU-khen im Va-GON er-LAUBT?

Wait, my luggage is still on board!
Warten Sie, mein Gepäck ist noch an Bord!
VAR-ten See, mighn Ge-PAEK ist nokh an Bord!

Where can I get a map?
Wo kann ich eine Karte bekommen?
Voh kann ikh IGH-ne KAR-te be-KO-men?

What zone is this?
Welche Zone ist das?
VEL-khe TSOH-ne ist das?

Please be careful of the gap!
Achtung, Lücke!
AKH-toong, LUE-ke!

I am about to run out of gas.
Mir geht der Treibstoff aus.
Meer gayt der TRIGHB-shtoff aus.

My tank is halfway full.
Mein Tank ist halbvoll.
Mighn Tank ist HALB-foll.

What type of gas does this car take?
Was tanke ich für dieses Auto?
Vas TAN-ke ikh fuer DEE-ses AU-to?

There is gas leaking out of my car.
Aus meinem Auto tritt Benzin aus.
Aus MIGH-nem AU-to tritt Ben-TSEEN aus.

Fill up the tank.
Füll den Tank auf.
Fuell den Tank auf.

There is no more gas in my car.
Der Tank ist leer.
Der Tank ist layr.

Where can I find the nearest gas station?
Wo ist die nächste Tankstelle?
Voh ist dee NAEKH-ste TANK-shtel-le?

The engine light for my car is on.
Die Motorkontrollleuchte meines Autos blinkt.
Dee MOH-tor-kon-TROLL-loykh-te MIGH-nes AU-tos blinkt.

Do you mind if I drive?
Macht es Ihnen etwas aus, wenn ich fahre?
Makht es EE-nen ET-was aus venn ikh FAH-re?

Please get in the back seat.
Bitte setz dich auf den Rücksitz.
BI-te sets dikh auf den RUEK-sits.

Let me get my bags out before you leave.
Lassen Sie mich meine Sachen herausnehmen, bevor Sie losfahren.
LA-ssen See mikh MIGH-ne SA-khen he-RAUS-nay-men, be-FOHR See LOHS-fah-ren.

The weather is bad, please drive slowly.
Das Wetter ist schlecht, bitte fahren Sie langsam.
Das VE-tter ist shlekht, BI-te FAH-ren See LANG-sam.

Our vehicle isn't equipped to travel there.
Mit unserem Fahrzeug kann man nicht dorthin fahren.
Mit UN-se-rem FAHR-tsoyg kann man nikht dort-HIN FAH-ren.

One ticket to the north, please.
Eine Fahrkarte Richtung Norden, bitte.
IGH-ne FAHR-kar-te RIKH-toong NOR-den, BI-te.

If you get lost, call me.
Rufen Sie mich an, wenn Sie sich verlaufen.
ROO-fen See mikh an, venn See sikh fer-LAU-fen.

That bus is overcrowded. I will wait for the next one.
Dieser Bus ist überfüllt. Ich werde auf den nächsten warten.
DEE-ser Bus ist ue-ber-FUELLT. IKH VAYR-de auf den NAEKH-sten VAR-ten.

Please, take my seat.
Bitte nehmen Sie meinen Platz.
BI-te NAY-men See MIGH-nen Plats.

Ma'am, I think your stop is coming up.
Entschuldigen Sie, ich glaube Ihr Halt kommt als Nächstes.
Ent-SHOOL-dee-gen See, ikh GLAU-be Eer Halt kommt als NAEKH-stes.

Wake me up when we get to our destination.
Wecken Sie mich, wenn wir ankommen.
VE-kken See mikh, venn veer AN-kom-men.

I would like to purchase a travel pass for the entire day.
Ich möchte gerne ein Tagesticket kaufen.
Ikh MOEKH-te GAYR-ne ighn TAH-ges-TI-kket KAU-fen.

Would you like to swap seats with me?
Möchten Sie die Plätze tauschen?
MOEKH-ten See dee PLAE-tse TAU-shen?

I want to sit with my family.
Ich möchte mit meiner Familie zusammensitzen.
Ikh MOEKH-te mit MIGH-ner Fa-MEE-lee-e tsoo-SAM-men SI-tsen.

I would like a window seat for this trip.
Ich möchte gerne einen Fensterplatz haben.
Ikh MOEKH-te GAYR-ne IGH-nen FEN-ster-plats HAH-ben.

RELIGIOUS QUESTIONS

Where can I go to pray?
Wo kann ich hier beten?
Voh kann ikh heer BAY-ten?

What services does your church offer?
Welche Dienste bietet Ihre Kirche an?
VEL-khe DEEN-ste BEE-tet EE-re KIR-khe an?

Are you non-denominational?
Sind Sie überkonfessionell?
Sind See UE-ber-kon-fes-see-o-NELL?

Is there a shuttle to your church?
Gibt es einen Shuttle-Bus zu Ihrer Kirche?
Geebt es IGH-nen SHUTTLE-bus tsoo EE-er KIR-khe?

How long does church last?
Wie lange dauert der Gottesdienst?
Vee LAN-ge DAU-ert der GOT-tes-deenst?

Where is your bathroom?
Wo ist Ihr Klo?
Voh ist Eer Kloh?

What should I wear to your services?
Was soll ich für Ihren Gottesdienst anziehen?
Vas soll ikh fuer EE-ren GOT-tes-deenst AN-tsee-hen?

Where is the nearest Catholic church?
Wo ist die nächste katholische Kirche?
Voh ist dee NAEKH-ste ka-TOH-lee-she KIR-khe?

Where is the nearest mosque?
Wo ist die nächste Moschee?
Voh ist dee NAEKH-ste Mo-SHAY?

Does your church perform weddings?
Bietet Ihre Kirche Hochzeiten an?
BEE-tet EE-re KIR-khe HOKH-tsigh-ten an?

Who is getting married?
Wer heiratet?
VAYR HIGH-rah-tet?

Will our marriage license be legal if we leave the country?
Wird unsere Ehe international anerkannt?
Vird UN-se-re AY-he IN-ter-na-tsee-o-NAHL AN-er-kannt?

Where do we get our marriage license?
Wo bekommen wir unsere Heiratsurkunde?
Voh be-KOM-men veer UN-se-re HIGH-rahts-oor-koon-de?

What is the charge for marrying us?
Was kostet es, hier zu heiraten?
Vas KOS-tet es, heer tsoo HIGH-ra-ten?

Do you handle same-sex marriage?
Nehmen Sie gleichgeschlechtliche Eheschließungen vor?
NAY-men See GLIGHKH-ge-shlekht-lee-khe AY-he-shlee-ssoong-en FOR?

Please gather here to pray.
Bitte versammeln Sie sich hier zum Gebet.
BI-te fer-SAM-meln See sikh heer tsoom Gay-BAYT.

I would like to lead a sermon.
Ich möchte gerne eine Predigt halten.
Ikh MOEKH-te GAYR-ne IGH-ne PRAY-digt HAL-ten.

I would like to help with prayer.
Ich möchte gerne beim Beten helfen.
Ikh MOEKH-te GAYR-ne bighm BAY-ten HEL-fen.

How should I dress before arriving?
Was soll ich anziehen?
Vas soll ikh AN-tsee-hen?

What are your rules?
Was sind Ihre Regeln?
Vas sind EE-re RAY-geln?

Are cell phones allowed in your building?
Sind Handys hier erlaubt?
Sind HAEN-dees heer er-LAUBT?

I plan on bringing my family this Sunday.
Ich werde am Sonntag meine Familie mitbringen.
Ikh VAYR-de am SONN-tag MIGH-ne Fa-MEE-lee-e MIT-bring-en.

Do you accept donations?
Akzeptieren Sie Spenden?
Ak-tsep-TEER-en See SHPEN-den?

I would like to offer my time to your cause.
Ich möchte mich freiwillig melden.
Ikh MOEKH-te mikh FRIGH-vil-lig MEL-den.

What book should I be reading from?
Aus welchem Buch soll ich lesen?
Aus VEL-khem Bookh soll ikh LAY-sen?

Do you have a gift store?
Haben Sie einen Souvenirladen?
HAH-ben See IGH-nen SOO-ve-neer-lah-den?

EMERGENCY

I need help over here!
Ich brauche Hilfe!
Ikh BRAU-khe HIL-fe!

I'm lost, please help me.
Ich habe mich verlaufen, bitte helfen Sie mir.
Ikh HAH-be mikh fer-LAU-fen, BI-te HEL-fen See meer.

Someone call the police!
Kann jemand die Polizei rufen!
Kann YAY-mand dee Po-lee-TSIGH ROO-fen!

Is there a lawyer who speaks English?
Gibt es hier einen englischsprachigen Anwalt?
Geebt es heer IGH-nen ENG-lish-SHPRAH-khi-gen AN-valt?

Please help, my car doesn't work.
Bitte helfen Sie mir, mein Auto ist kaputt.
BI-te HEL-fen See meer, mighn AU-to ist ka-PUTT.

There was a collision!
Da war ein Unfall!
Da vahr ighn UN-fall!

Call an ambulance!
Rufen Sie den Rettungswagen!
ROO-fen See den RET-toongs-wah-gen!

Am I under arrest?
Bin ich verhaftet?
Bin ikh fer-HAF-tet?

I need an interpreter, this is an emergency!
Ich brauche einen Übersetzer, das ist ein Notfall!
Ikh BRAU-khe IGH-nen Ue-ber-SETS-er, das ist ighn NOHT-fall!

My back hurts.
Mein Rücken tut weh.
Mighn RUE-kken toot vay.

Is there an American consulate here?
Gibt es hier eine amerikanische Botschaft?
Geebt es heer IGH-ne a-mer-ee-KAHN-ee-she BOHT-shaft?

I'm sick and don't feel too well.
Ich bin krank und fühle mich schlecht.
Ikh bin krank oond FUE-le mikh shlekht.

Is there a pharmacy where I can get medicine?
Gibt es hier eine Apotheke?
Geebt es heer IGH-ne A-po-TAY-ke?

I need a doctor immediately.
Ich brauche sofort einen Arzt.
Ikh BRAU-che so-FORT IGH-nen Artst.

I have a tooth missing.
Mir fehlt ein Zahn.
Meer faylt ighn Tsahn.

Please! Someone bring my child to me!
Kann mir bitte jemand mein Kind herbringen?
Kann meer BI-te YAY-mand mighn Kind HAYR-bring-en?

Where does it hurt?
Wo tut es weh?
Voh toot es vay?

Hold on to me!
Halten Sie sich fest!
HAL-ten See sikh fest!

There's an emergency!
Es ist ein Notfall!
Es ist ighn NOHT-fall!

I need a telephone to call for help.
Ich brauche ein Telefon, um Hilfe zu holen.
Ikh BRAU-khe ighn TAY-le-fon, um HIL-fe tsoo HOH-len.

My nose is bleeding.
Meine Nase blutet.
MIGH-ne NAH-se BLOO-tet.

I twisted my ankle.
Ich habe mir den Knöchel verstaucht.
Ikh HAH-be meer den KNOE-khel fer-SHTAUKHT.

I don't feel so good.
Mir geht es nicht gut.
Meer gayt es nikht goot.

Don't move, please.
Bewegen Sie sich bitte nicht.
Be-VAY-gen See sikh BI-te nikht.

Hello operator, can I place a collect call?
Hallo, kann ich ein R-Gespräch führen?
HA-lo, kann ikh ighn ER-Ge-SHPRAEKH FUE-ren?

I'll get a doctor for you.
Ich rufe Ihnen einen Arzt.
Ikh ROO-fe EE-nen IGH-nen Artst.

Please hold my passports for a while.
Bitte halten Sie kurz meinen Pass.
BI-te HAL-ten See koorts MIGH-nen Pass.

I lost my wallet.
Ich habe meine Brieftasche verloren.
Ikh HAH-be MIGH-ne BREEF-ta-sheh fer-LOH-ren.

I have a condition! Please check my wallet.
Ich bin chronisch krank! Bitte sehen Sie in meiner Brieftasche nach.
Ikh bin KROH-nish krank! BI-te SAY-hen See in MIGH-ner BREEF-ta-sheh nakh.

My wife is in labor, please help!
Meine Frau liegt in den Wehen, bitte helfen Sie mir!
MIGH-ne Frau leegt in dayn VAY-hen, BI-te HEL-fen See meer!

I would like to talk to my lawyer.
Ich möchte meinen Anwalt sprechen.
Ikh MOEKH-te MIGH-nen AN-valt SHPRE-khen.

It's an earthquake!
Es ist ein Erdbeben!
Es ist ighn AYRD-bay-ben!

Get under the desk and protect your head.
Unter den Tisch, schützen Sie Ihren Kopf.
UN-ter den Tish, SHUE-tsen See EE-ren Kopf.

How can I help you?
Wie kann ich Ihnen helfen?
Vee kann ikh EE-nen HEL-fen?

Everyone, he needs help!
Hey, er braucht Hilfe!
Hey, er braukht HIL-fe!

Yes, help me get an ambulance.
Ja, bitte helfen Sie mir den Rettungswagen zu rufen.
Ya, BI-te HEL-fen See meer den RET-toongs-wah-gen tsoo ROO-fen.

Thank you, but I am fine. Please don't help me.
Danke, mir geht's gut. Sie brauchen mir nicht zu helfen.
DAN-ke, meer gayts goot. See BRAU-khen meer nikht tsoo HEL-fen.

I need help carrying this injured person.
Ich brauche Hilfe, um diese Person zu tragen.
Ikh BRAU-che HIL-fe, um DEE-se Per-SOHN tsoo TRAH-gen.

TECHNOLOGY

What is the country's official website?
Was ist die offizielle Webseite dieses Landes?
Vas ist dee OF-fee-tsee-EL-le VEB-sigh-te DEE-ses LAN-des?

Do you know the name of a good wi-fi café?
Kennen Sie ein gutes Internetcafé?
KEN-nen See ighn GOO-tes IN-ter-net-ka-FAY?

Do you have any experience with computers?
Kennen Sie sich mit Computern aus?
KEN-nen See sikh mit Komp-YOO-tern aus?

How well do you know Apple products?
Wie gut kennen Sie sich mit Apple-Produkten aus?
Vee goot KEN-nen See sikh mit AP-ple-Pro-DOOK-ten aus?

What kind of work did you do with computers?
Inwiefern haben Sie schon mit Computern gearbeitet?
In-wee-FERN HAH-ben See shohn mit Komp-YOO-tern ge-AR-bigh-tet?

Are you a programmer?
Sind Sie ein Programmierer?
Sind See ighn Pro-gra-MEER-er?

Are you a developer?
Sind Sie ein Entwickler?
Sind See ighn Ent-vik-kler?

I want to use this computer instead of that one.
Ich würde gerne stattdessen diesen Computer verwenden.
Ikh WUER-de GAYRN-ne statt-DES-sen DEE-sen Komp-YOO-ter fer-VEN-den.

Do you know where I can buy discount computer parts?
Wissen Sie, wo ich günstige Computer-Hardware kaufen kann?
VI-ssen See, wo ikh GUENS-stee-ge Komp-YOO-ter-Hard-vayr KAU-fen kann?

I have ten years of experience with Windows.
Ich habe zehn Jahre Erfahrung mit Windows.
Ikh HAH-be tsayn YAH-re Er-FAH-roong mit Win-dows.

What is the wi-fi password?
Wie lautet das WLAN-Passwort?
Vee LAU-tet das VEH-Lahn-PASS-vort?

I need to have my login information reset.
Ich möchte meinen Account resetten.
Ikh MOEKH-te MIGH-nen Ak-KAUNT ree-SET-ten.

The hard drive is making a clicking noise.
Die Festplatte macht Klick-Geräusche.
Dee FEST-pla-tte makht KLIKK-Gay-ROY-she.

How do I uninstall this program from my device?
Wie deinstalliere ich das wieder?
Vee DAY-in-shtah-lee-re ikh das vee-der?

Can you help me set up a new account with this website?
Können Sie mir helfen, einen neuen Account auf dieser Webseite anzulegen?
KOEN-nen See meer HEL-fen, IGH-nen NOY-en Ak-KAUNT auf DEE-ser VEB-sigh-te AN-tsoo-lay-gen?

Why is the internet so slow?
Warum ist das Internet so langsam?
VAH-rum ist das IN-ter-net so LANG-sam?

Why is YouTube buffering every video I play?
Warum buffert YouTube jedes Video, das ich abspiele?
VAH-rum BAF-fert YOO-Toob YAY-des VEE-de-o, das ikh AB-shpee-le?

My web camera isn't displaying a picture.
Meine Webcam zeigt kein Bild an.
MIGH-ne VEB-kaem tsighgt kighn Bild an.

I have no bars on my phone.
Ich habe keinen Empfang auf meinem Handy.
Ikh HAH-be KIGH-nen Em-PFANG auf MIGH-nem HAEN-dee.

Where can I get my phone serviced?
Wo kann ich mein Handy reparieren lassen?
Voh kann ikh mighn HAEN-dee re-pah-REE-ren LAS-sen?

My phone shows that it is charging but won't charge.
Mein Handy zeigt an, dass es lädt, aber es lädt nicht.
Mighn HAEN-dee tsighgt an dass es laet, AH-ber es laet nikht.

I think someone else is controlling my computer.
Ich glaube, jemand anderes überwacht meinen Computer.
Ikh GLAU-be YAY-mand AN-de-res ue-ber-WAKHT MIGH-nen Komp-YOO-ter.

My computer just gave a blue screen and shut down.
Mein Computer hatte einen Bluescreen und hat sich ausgeschaltet.
Mighn Komp-YOO-ter HA-te IGH-nen BLOO-skreen oond hat sikh AUS-ge-shal-tet.

Do you have the battery for this laptop?
Haben Sie einen Akku für diesen Laptop?
HAH-ben See IGH-nen AH-koo fuer DEE-sen LAP-top.

Where can I get a compatible adapter?
Wo kann ich einen passenden Adapter bekommen?
Voh kann ikh IGH-nen PA-ssen-den A-DAP-ter bay-KOM-men?

I can't get online with the information you gave me.
Ich komme damit nicht ins Internet.
Ikh KOM-me DAH-mit nikht ins IN-ter-net.

This keyboard is not working correctly.
Diese Tastatur funktioniert nicht richtig.
DEE-se Tas-ta-TOOE foonk-tsee-o-NEERT nikht RIKH-tig.

What is the login information for this computer?
Was sind die Anmeldedaten für diesen Computer?
Vas sind dee AN-mel-de-da-ten fuer DEE-sen Komp-YOO-ter?

I need you to update my computer.
Bitte updaten Sie meinen Computer.
BI-te AP-dae-ten See MIGH-nen Komp-YOO-ter.

Can you build my website?
Können Sie mir eine Webseite erstellen?
KOEN-nen See meer IGH-ne VEB-sigh-te er-SHTEL-len?

I prefer Wordpress.
Ich bevorzuge Wordpress.
Ikh be-FOR-tsoo-ge VOERD-press.

What are your rates per hour?
Was kosten Sie pro Stunde?
Vas KOS-ten See proh SHTOON-de?

Do you have experience handling email servers?
Haben Sie Vorerfahrungen mit E-Mail-Servern?
HAH-ben See FOHR-er-fah-roong-en mit E-Mail-SER-vern?

I am locked out of my account, can you help?
Ich komme nicht in meinen Account, können Sie mir helfen?
Ikh KOM-me nikht in MIGH-nen Ak-KAUNT, KOEN-nen See meer HEL-fen?

None of the emails I am sending are going through.
Meine E-Mails kommen nicht an.
MIGH-ne E-Mails KOM-men nikht an.

The time and date on my computer are wrong.
Datum und Zeit auf meinem Computer sind falsch.
DAH-tum oond Tsight auf MIGH-nem Komp-YOO-ter sind falsh.

Is this game free to play?
Ist das Spiel gratis?
Ist das Shpeel GRAH-tis?

Where do I go to download the client?
Wo lade ich mir den Client herunter?
Voh LAH-de ikh meer den KLIGH-ent her-UN-ter?

I am having troubles chatting with my family.
Ich habe Schwierigkeiten, mit meiner Familie zu chatten.
Ikh HAH-be SHVEE-rig-kighi-ten, meet MIGH-ner Fah-MEE-lee-e tsoo TSHAET-ten.

Is this the fastest computer here?
Ist das der schnellste Computer hier?
Ist das der SHNELL-ste Komp-YOO-ter heer?

How much space is on the computer?
Wie viel Speicherplatz hat der Computer?
Vee feel SHPIGH-kher-plats hat der Komp-YOO-ter?

Will my profile be deleted once I log out? Or does it save?
Bleibt mein Profil auch nach dem Ausloggen noch gespeichert?
Blighbt mighn Pro-FEEL aukh nakh dem AUS-log-gen nokh ge-SHPIGH-khert?

How much do you charge for computer use?
Wie viel kostet es, einen Computer zu benutzen?
Vee-FEEL KOS-tet es, IGH-nen Komp-YOO-ter tsoo be-NOO-tsen?

Are group discounts offered?
Gibt es Gruppenrabatte?
Geebt es GRU-pen-ra-BAT-te?

Can I use my own headphones with your computer?
Kann ich meine eigenen Kopfhörer für den Computer benutzen?
Kann ikh migh-ne IGH-ge-nen KOPF-hoe-rer fuer den Komp-YOO-ter be-NOO-tsen?

Do you have a data cap?
Haben Sie ein Datenlimit?
HAH-ben See ighn DAH-ten-li-mit?

I think this computer has a virus.
Ich glaube, der Computer hat einen Virus.
Ikh GLAU-be, der Komp-YOO-ter hat IGH-nen VEE-rus.

The battery for my laptop is running low.
Die Batterie von meinem Laptop ist fast leer.
Dee Bah-ter-REE fon MIGH-nem LAP-top ist fast layr.

Where can I plug this in? I need to recharge my device.
Wo kann ich das einstecken? Ich muss mein Gerät aufladen.
Voh kann ikh das IGHN-shtek-ken? Ikh muss mighn Ge-RAET AUF-la-den.

Do you have a mini-USB cord?
Haben Sie einen Mini-USB-Stecker?
HAH-ben See IGH-nen MEE-nee-USB-Shtek-ker?

Where can I go to watch the game?
Wo kann ich das Spiel ansehen?
Voh kann ikh das Shpeel AN-se-hen?

Do you have an iPhone charger?
Haben Sie ein iPhone-Ladekabel?
HAH-ben See ighn IGH-Fohn-LAH-de-kah-bel?

I need a new battery for my watch.
Ich brauche eine neue Batterie für meine Uhr.
Ikh BRAU-che IGH-ne NOY-e Bah-te-REE fuer MIGH-ne Oor.

I need to borrow an HDMI cord.
Ich muss mir ein HDMI-Kabel ausborgen.
Ikh muss meer ighn Ha-De-Em-Ee-KAH-bel AUS-bor-gen.

What happens when I exceed the data cap?
Was passiert, wenn ich das Datenlimit überschreite?
Vas pa-SEERT, venn ikh das DAH-ten-li-mit ue-ber-SHRIGH-te?

Can you help me pair my Bluetooth device?
Können Sie mir helfen, mein Bluetooth-Gerät zu verbinden?
KOE-nen See meer HEL-fen, mighn BLOO-toof-Gay-raet tsoo fer-BIN-den?

I need a longer ethernet cord.
Ich brauche ein längeres Internetkabel.
Ikh BRAU-che ighn LAEN-ge-res IN-ter-net-kah-bel.

Why is this website restricted?
Warum ist diese Webseite gesperrt?
Vah-RUM ist DEE-se VEB-sigh-te ge-SHPERRT?

How can I unblock this website?
Wie kann ich diese Webseite entsperren?
Vee kann ikh DEE-se VEB-sigh-te ent-SHPER-ren?

Is that television 4k or higher?
Hat dieser Fernseher 4k oder mehr?
Hat DEE-ser FERN-say-her 4k OH-der mayr?

Do you have the Office suite on this computer?
Hat dieser Computer Office?
Hat DEE-ser Komp-YOO-ter OF-fis?

This application won't install on my device.
Diese Anwendung lässt sich auf meinem Gerät nicht installieren.
DEE-se AN-ven-doong laesst sikh auf MIGH-nem Ge-RAET nikht in-shtah-LEE-ren.

Can you change the channel on the television?
Können Sie den Fernsehsender wechseln?
KOE-nen See den FERN-say-SEN-der WEKH-seln?

I think a fuse blew.
Ich glaube, eine Sicherung ist durchgebrannt.
Ikh GLAU-be, IGH-ne SI-kher-oong ist DURKH-ge-brannt.

The screen is black and won't come on.
Der Bildschirm ist schwarz und geht nicht an.
Der BILD-shirm ist shvarts oond gayt nikht an.

I keep getting pop-ups on every website.
Ich bekomme ständig Pop-ups auf jeder Webseite.
Ikh be-KOM-me SHTAEN-dig POP-aps auf YAY-der VEB-sigh-te.

This computer is moving much slower than it should.
Der Computer ist viel langsamer, als er sein sollte.
Der Komp-YOO-ter ist feel LANG-sah-mer als er sighn SOLL-te.

I need to reactivate my copy of Windows.
Ich muss Windows noch einmal aktivieren.
Ikh muss VIN-dows nokh IGHN-mal ak-tee-VEE-ren.

Why is this website blocked on my laptop?
Warum wird diese Webseite auf meinem Laptop geblockt?
VAH-rum vird DEE-se VEB-sigh-te auf MIGH-nem LAP-top ge-BLOKKT?

Can you show me how to download videos to my computer?
Können Sie mir zeigen, wie ich Videos auf meinen Computer
herunterlade?
KOE-nen See meer TSIGH-gen, vee ikh VEE-de-os auf MIGH-nen Komp-YOO-ter he-ROON-ter lah-de?

Can I insert a flash drive into this computer?
Kann ich einen USB-Stick in diesen Computer stecken?
Kann ikh IGH-nen USB-SHTIKK in dee-sen Komp-YOO-ter SHTEK-ken?

I want to change computers.
Ich möchte einen anderen Computer.
IKH MOEKH-te IGH-nen AN-de-ren Komp-YOO-ter.

Is Chrome the only browser I can use with this computer?
Kann ich auf diesem Computer nur Chrome nutzen?
Kann ikh auf DEE-sem Komp-YOO-ter noor Krohm NOO-tsen?

Do you track my usage on any of these devices?
Werden meine Aktivitäten auf einem dieser Geräte von Ihnen
nachverfolgt?
VAYR-den MIGH-ne Akt-ee-vee-TAE-ten auf IGH-nem DEE-ser Ge-RAE-te fon EE-nen NAKH-fer-folgt?

CONVERSATION TIPS

Pardon me.
Entschuldigen Sie bitte.
Ent-SHOOL-dee-gen See BI-te.

Please speak more slowly.
Bitte sprechen Sie langsamer.
BI-te SHPRE-khen See LANG-sa-mer.

I don't understand.
Ich verstehe nicht.
Ikh fer-SHTAY-he nikht.

Can you say that more clearly?
Können Sie das noch einmal wiederholen?
KOE-nen See das nokh IGHN-mal vee-der-HOH-len?

I don't speak Spanish very well.
Ich spreche nicht gut Spanisch.
Ikh SHPRE-khe nikht goot SHPAH-nish.

Can you please translate that to English for me?
Können Sie mir das bitte auf Englisch übersetzen?
KOE-nen See meer das BI-te auf ENG-lish ue-ber-SET-sen?

Let's talk over there where it is quieter.
Lass uns dort drüben sprechen, wo es leiser ist.
Lass uns dort DRUE-ben SHPRE-khen, voh es LIGH-ser ist.

Sit down over there.
Setz dich dort drüben hin.
Sets dikh dort DRUE-ben hin.

May I?
Darf ich?
Darf ikh?

I am from America.
Ich bin aus den USA.
Ikh bin aus den OO-Es-AH.

Am I talking too much?
Rede ich zu viel?
RAY-de ikh tsoo feel?

I speak your language badly.
Ich spreche Ihre Sprache nur schlecht.
Ikh SHPRE-khe EE-re SHPRAH-khe noor shlekht.

Am I saying that word correctly?
Habe ich das Wort korrekt ausgesprochen?
HAH-be ikh das Vort ko-REKT AUS-ge-shpro-khen?

You speak English very well.
Sie sprechen sehr gut Englisch.
See SHPRE-khen sayr goot ENG-lish.

This is my first time in your lovely country.
Ich bin zum ersten Mal in Ihrem wunderbaren Land.
Ikh bin tsoom ersten Mahl in EE-rem VOON-der-bah-ren Land.

Write that information down on this piece of paper.
Schreiben Sie diese Information bitte auf dieses Stück Papier.
SHRIGH-ben See DEE-se In-for-ma-tsee-OHN BI-te auf DEE-ses Shtuek Pa-PEER.

Do you understand?
Verstehen Sie mich?
Fer-SHTAY-hen See mikh?

How do you pronounce that word?
Wie spricht man dieses Wort aus?
Vee SHPRIKHT man DEE-ses Vort aus?

Is this how you write this word?
Schreibt man dieses Wort so?
Shrighbt man DEE-ses Vort soh?

Can you give me an example?
Können Sie mir ein Beispiel geben?
KOE-nen See meer ighn BIGH-shpeel gay-ben?

Wait a moment, please.

Warten Sie bitte einen Moment.

Var-ten See BI-te IGH-nen Mo-MENT.

If there is anything you want, tell me.

Wenn Sie etwas brauchen, sagen Sie es einfach.

Venn See ET-was BRAU-khen, SAH-gen See es IGHN-fach.

I don't want to bother you anymore, so I will go.

Ich möchte Sie nicht weiter stören, darum gehe ich jetzt.

Ikh MOEKH-te See nikht VIGH-ter SHTOE-ren, DAH-room GAY-he ikh yetst.

Please take care of yourself.

Bitte passen Sie auf sich auf.

BI-te PAS-sen See auf sikh auf.

When you arrive, let us know.

Melden Sie sich, wenn Sie ankommen.

MEL-den See sikh, venn See AN-kom-men.

DATE NIGHT

What is your telephone number?
Ist das deine Telefonnummer?
Ist das DIGH-ne Te-le-FOHN-noom-mer?

I'll call you for the next date.
Ich rufe dich noch wegen unserem nächsten Treffen an.
Ikh ROO-fe dikh nokh VAY-gen UN-se-rem NAEKH-sten TREF-fen an.

I had a good time, can't wait to see you again.
Ich habe es sehr genossen mit dir und freue mich darauf, dich
wiederzusehen.
*Ikh HAH-be es sayr ge-NOS-sen mit deer oond FROY-e mikh da-RAUF,
dikh VEE-der-tsoo-say-hen.*

I'll pay for dinner tonight.
Ich zahle heute das Abendessen.
Ikh TSAH-le HOY-te das AH-bend-es-sen.

Dinner at my place?
Abendessen bei mir?
AH-bend-es-sen bigh meer?

I don't think we should see each other anymore.
Ich glaube, wir sollten uns nicht mehr sehen.
Ikh GLAU-be veer SOL-lten uns nikht mayr SAY-hen.

I'm afraid this will be the last time we see each other.
Es tut mir leid, aber heute werden wir uns zum letzten Mal sehen.
*Es toot meer lighd, AH-ber HOY-te VAYR-den veer oons tsoom LET-sten
Mahl SAY-hen.*

You look fantastic.
Du siehst fantastisch aus.
Doo seest fan-TAS-teesh aus.

Would you like to dance with me?
Möchtest du mit mir tanzen?
MOEKH-test doo mit meer TAN-tsen?

Are there any 3D cinemas in this city?
Gibt es hier irgendwo in der Stadt 3D-Kinos?
Geebt es heer IR-gend-woh in der Shtat 3-Day-Kee-nos?

We should walk along the beach.
Wir sollten am Strand entlanglaufen.
Veer SOLL-ten am Shtrand ent-LANG-lau-fen.

I hope you like my car.
Ich hoffe, dir gefällt mein Auto.
Ikh HOF-fe, deer ge-FAE-lt mighn AU-to.

What movies are playing today?
Welche Filme werden heute gespielt?
VEL-khe FIL-me VAYR-den HOY-te ge-SHPEELT?

I've seen this film, but I wouldn't mind watching it again.
Ich kenne diesen Film schon, aber ich schaue ihn mir gerne noch einmal an.
Ikh KEN-ne DEE-sen Film shohn, AH-ber ikh SHAU-e een meer GAYR-ne nokh IGHN-mal an.

Do you know how to do the salsa?
Kannst du Salsa tanzen?
Kannst doo SAL-sa TAN-tsen?

We can dance all night.
Wir können die ganze Nacht durchtanzen.
Veer KOEN-nen dee GAN-tse Nakht DOORKH-tan-tsen.

I have some friends that will be joining us tonight.
Einige Freunde von mir werden heute Abend mitkommen.
IGH-nee-ge FROYN-de fon meer VAYR-den HOY-te AH-bend MIT-kom-men.

Is this a musical or a regular concert?
Ist das ein Musical oder ein normales Konzert?
Ist das ighn MOO-see-kal OH-der ighn nor-MAH-les Kon-TSERT?

Did you get VIP tickets?
Hast du VIP-Tickets bekommen?
Hast doo Vee-Igh-Pee-TI-kkets be-KOM-men?

I'm going to have to cancel on you tonight. Maybe another time?
Ich kann heute Abend doch nicht. Vielleicht ein anderes Mal?
Ikh kann HOY-te AH-bend dokh nikht. Fee-LIGHKHT ighn AN-de-res Mahl?

If you want, we can go to your place.
Wir können zu dir gehen, wenn du willst.
Veer KOEN-nen tsoo deer GAY-hen, venn doo villst.

I'll pick you up tonight.
Ich hole dich heute Abend ab.
Ikh HOH-le dikh HOY-te AH-bend ab.

This one is for you!
Das ist für dich!
Das ist fuer dikh!

What time does the party start?
Wann startet die Party?
Vann SHTAR-tet dee PAR-tee?

Will it end on time or will you have to leave early?
Wird es pünktlich aufhören oder musst du früher gehen?
Vird es PUNKT-likh AUF-hoe-ren OH-der musst doo FRUE-her GAY-hen?

Did you like your gift?
Magst du dein Geschenk?
Mahgst doo dighn Ge-SHENK?

I want to invite you to watch a movie with me tonight.
Wollen wir heute gemeinsam einen Film anschauen?
VOL-len veer HOY-te ge-MIGHN-sam IGH-nen Film AN-shau-en.

Do you want anything to drink?
Möchtest du etwas zu trinken?
MOEKH-test doo ET-was tsoo TRIN-ken?

I am twenty-six years old.
Ich bin sechsundzwanzig Jahre alt.
Ikh bin SEKHS-oond-tsvahn-tsig YAH-re alt.

You're invited to a small party I'm having at my house.
Du bist zu einer kleinen Feier bei mir zuhause eingeladen.
Doo bist tsoo IGH-ner KLIGH-nen FIGH-er bigh meer tsoo-HAU-se IGHN-ge-la-den.

I love you.
Ich liebe dich.
Ikh LEE-be dikh.

We should go to the arcade.
Wir sollten in die Spielhalle gehen.
Veer SOLL-ten in dee SHPEEL-hal-le GAY-hen.

Have you ever played this game before?
Hast du dieses Spiel schon einmal gespielt?
Hast doo DEE-ses Shpeel shohn IGHN-mal ge-SHPEELT?

Going on this ferry would be really romantic.
Mit der Fähre zu fahren wäre sehr romantisch.
Mit der FAE-re tsoo FAH-ren VAE-re sayr ro-MAN-tish.

How about a candlelight dinner?
Wie wäre es mit einem Abendessen bei Kerzenlicht?
Vee vae-re es mit IGH-nem AH-bend-es-sen bigh KER-tsen-likht?

Let's dance and sing!
Lass uns tanzen und singen!
Lass uns TAN-tsen oond SING-en!

Will you marry me?
Willst du mich heiraten?
Vill-st doo mikh HIGH-rah-ten?

Set the table, please.
Deck bitte den Tisch.
Deck BI-te den Tish.

Here are the dishes and the glasses.
Hier sind Geschirr und Gläser.
Heer sind Ge-SHIRR oond GLAE-ser.

Where is the cutlery?
Wo ist das Besteck?
Voh ist das Be-SHTEKK?

May I hold your hand?
Kann ich deine Hand halten?
Kann ikh digh-ne Hand HAL-ten?

Let me get that for you.
Lass mich das für dich holen.
Lass mikh das fuer dikh HOH-len.

I think our song is playing!
Ich glaube, das ist unser Lied!
ikh GLAU-be, das ist UN-ser Leed!

Let's make a wish together.
Lass uns gemeinsam etwas wünschen.
Lass uns ge-MIGHN-sam ET-vas VUEN-shen.

Is there anything that you want from me?
Brauchst du etwas von mir?
Braukhst doo ET-vas fon meer?

There is nowhere I would rather be than right here with you.
Es gibt keinen Ort auf der Welt, an dem ich gerade lieber wäre als hier mit dir.
Es geebt KIGH-nen Ort auf der Velt, an dem ikh ge-RAH-de LEE-ber VAE-re als heer mit deer.

I'll give you a ride back to your place.
Ich bringe dich nach Hause.
Ikh BRING-e dikh nakh HAU-se.

Would you like me to hold your purse?
Soll ich dir deine Tasche tragen?
Soll ikh deer DIGH-ne TA-she TRAH-gen?

Let's pray before we eat our meal.
Lass uns vor dem Essen beten.
Lass uns for dem ES-sen BAY-ten.

Do you need a napkin?
Brauchst du eine Serviette?
Braukhst doo IGH-ne Ser-vee-ET-te?

I'm thirsty.
Ich habe Durst.
Ikh HAH-be Doorst.

I hope you enjoy your meal.
Ich hoffe, es schmeckt dir.
Ikh HOF-fe, es shmekkt deer.

I need to add more salt to the salt shaker.
Ich muss das Salz im Streuer nachfüllen.
Ikh muss das Salts im SHTROY-er NAKH-fuel-len.

We should get married!
Wir sollten heiraten!
Veer SOLL-ten HIGH-rah-ten!

How old are you?
Wie alt bist du?
Vee alt bist doo?

Will you dream of me?
Wirst du von mir träumen?
Virst doo fon meer TROY-men?

Thank you very much for the wonderful date last night.
Danke für das wunderbare Date letzte Nacht.
DAN-ke fuer das VOON-der-bah-re Dayt LET-ste Nakht.

Would you like to come to a party this weekend?
Möchtest du dieses Wochenende zu einer Party kommen?
MOEKH-test doo DEE-ses VO-khen-en-de tsoo IGH-ner PAR-tee KOM-men?

This Saturday night, right?
Diesen Samstag, oder?
DEE-sen SAMS-tahg, OH-der?

I will be lonely without you.
Ich werde dich vermissen.
Ikh VAYR-de dikh fer-MIS-sen.

Please stay the night.
Bitte bleib heute Nacht bei mir.
BI-te blighb HOY-te Nakht bigh meer.

I like your fragrance.
Ich mag dein Parfüm.
Ikh mahg dighn Par-FUEM.

That is a beautiful outfit you're wearing.
Das ist ein wunderschönes Outfit, das du trägst.
Das ist ighn VOON-der-SHOE-nes AUT-fit, das doo traegst.

You look beautiful.
Du siehst wunderschön aus.
Doo seest VOON-der-shoen aus.

Let me help you out of the car.
Lass mich dir aus dem Auto helfen.
Lass mikh deer aus dem AU-to HEL-fen.

Sarah, will you come with me to dinner?
Sarah, gehst du mit mir Abendessen?
SAH-rah, gayst doo mit meer AH-bend-es-sen?

I would like to ask you out on a date.
Ich möchte gerne mit dir ausgehen.
Ikh MOEKH-te GAYR-ne mit deer AUS-gay-hen.

Are you free tonight?
Hast du heute Abend Zeit?
Hast doo HOY-te AH-bend Tsight?

This is my phone number. Call me anytime.
Das ist meine Telefonnummer. Ruf mich jederzeit an.
Das ist MIGH-ne Te-le-FON-num-mer. Roof mikh YE-der-tsight an.

Can I hug you?
Darf ich dich umarmen?
Darf ikh deech um-AR-men?

Would you like to sing karaoke?
Möchtest du Karaoke singen?
MOEKH-test doo Ka-ra-OH-ke SING-en?

What kind of song would you like to sing?
Welche Art von Lied möchtest du gerne singen?
VEL-khe Art von Leed MOEKH-test doo GAYR-ne SING-en?

Have you ever sung this song before?
Hast du dieses Lied schon mal gesungen?
Hast doo DEE-ses Leed shohn mahl ge-SOON-gen?

We can sing it together.
Wir können es gemeinsam singen.
Veer KOEN-nen es ge-MIGHN-sam SING-gen.

Can I kiss you?
Darf ich dich küssen?
Darf ikh dikh KUES-sen?

Are you cold?
Ist dir kalt?
Ist deer kalt?

We can stay out as late as you want.
Wir können so lange bleiben, wie du willst.
Veer KOEN-nen so LAN-ge BLIGH-ben, vee doo villst.

Please, dinner is on me.
Lass nur, ich bezahle heute.
Lass noor, ikh be-TSAH-le HOY-te.

Shall we split the bill?
Sollen wir die Rechnung aufteilen?
SOL-len veer dee REKH-noong AUF-tigh-len?

We should spend more time together.
Wir sollten mehr Zeit miteinander verbringen.
Veer SOLL-ten mayr Tsight MIT-igh-nan-der fer-BRING-en.

We should walk the town tonight.
Wir sollten heute Abend durch die Stadt gehen.
Veer SOLL-ten HOY-te AH-bend doorkh dee Shtat GAY-hen.

Did you enjoy everything?
Hat es dir gefallen?
Hat es deer ge-FAL-len?

MONEY AND SHOPPING

May I try this on?
Darf ich das anprobieren?
Darf ikh das AN-pro-bee-ren?

How much does this cost?
Was kostet das?
Vas KOS-tet das?

Do I sign here or here?
Wo soll ich unterschreiben?
Voh soll ikh un-ter-SHRIGH-ben?

Is that your final price?
Ist das Ihr letzter Preis?
Ist das Eer LETS-ter Prighs?

Where do I find toiletries?
Wo finde ich Toilettenartikel?
Voh FIN-de ikh To-ee-LET-ten-ar-TEE-kel?

Would you be willing to take five dollars for this item?
Bekomme ich das für fünf Dollar?
Be-KOM-me ikh das fuer fuenf DOL-lar?

I can't afford it at that price.
Das kann ich mir für den Preis nicht leisten.
Das kann ikh meer fuer den Prighs nikht LIGH-sten.

I can find this cheaper somewhere else.
Das finde ich woanders günstiger.
Das FIN-de ikh vo-AN-ders GUENS-tee-ger.

Is there a way we can haggle on price?
Ist das noch verhandelbar?
Ist das nokh fer-HAN-del-bar?

How many of these have sold today?
Wie viele von denen haben Sie heute schon verkauft?
Vee FEE-le fon DAY-nen HAH-ben See HOY-te shohn fer-KAUFT?

Can you wrap that up as a gift?
Können Sie das als Geschenk verpacken?
KOEN-nen See das als Ge-SHENK fer-PAK-ken?

Do you provide personalized letters?
Bieten Sie auch personalisierte Briefkarten an?
BEE-ten See aukh per-so-nal-ee-SEER-te BREEF-kar-ten an?

I would like this to be special delivered to my hotel.
Ich möchte das bitte extra an mein Hotel liefern lassen.
Ikh MOEKH-te das BI-te EKS-tra an mighn Ho-TEL LEE-fern LAS-sen.

Can you help me, please?
Können Sie mir bitte helfen?
KOE-nen See meer BI-te HEL-fen?

We should go shopping at the market.
Wir sollten auf dem Markt einkaufen.
Veer SOLL-ten auf dem Markt IGHN-kau-fen.

Are you keeping track of the clothes that fit me?
Merkst du dir die Kleidungsstücke, die mir passen?
Merkst doo deer dee KLIGH-doongs-shtue-ke, dee meer PAS-sen?

Can I have one size up?
Haben Sie das auch eine Nummer größer?
HAH-ben See das aukh IGH-ne NUM-mer GROE-sser?

How many bathrooms does the apartment have?
Wie viele Badezimmer hat das Apartment?
Vee FEE-le BAH-de-tsim-mer hat das A-PART-ment?

Where's the kitchen?
Wo ist die Küche?
Voh ist dee KUE-khe?

Does this apartment have a gas or electric stove?
Hat diese Wohnung einen Gasherd oder einen elektrischen Herd?
Hat DEE-se VOH-noong IGH-nen GAHS-herd OH-der IGH-nen e-LEK-tree-shen Herd?

Is there a spacious backyard?
Gibt es einen großen Hinterhof?
Geebt es IGH-nen GROH-ssen HIN-ter-hof?

How much is the down payment?
Wie hoch ist die Anzahlung?
VEE hokh ist dee AN-tsah-loong?

I'm looking for a furnished apartment.
Ich suche nach einer möblierten Wohnung.
Ikh SOO-khe nakh IGH-ner moe-LEER-ten VOH-noong.

I need a two-bedroom apartment to rent.
Ich möchte eine Wohnung mit zwei Schlafzimmern mieten.
Ikh MOEKH-te IGH-ne VOH-noong mit tsvigh SHLAF-tsim-mern MEE-ten.

I'm looking for an apartment with utilities paid.
Ich suche nach einer Wohnung mit inkludierten Nebenkosten.
Ikh SOO-khe nakh IGH-ner VOH-noong mit in-kloo-DEER-ten NAY-ben-kos-ten.

The carpet in this apartment needs to be pulled up.
Der Teppich in dieser Wohnung muss raus.
Der TEP-pikh in dee-ser VOH-noong muss raus.

I need you to come down on the price of this apartment.
Der Preis dieser Wohnung ist mir noch zu teuer.
Der Prighs dee-ser VOH-noong ist meer nokh tsoo TOY-er.

Will I be sharing this place with other people?
Werden dort auch andere wohnen?
VAYR-den dort aukh AN-de-re VOH-nen?

How do you work the fireplace?
Wie funktioniert der Kamin?
Vee funk-tsee-o-NEERT der Ka-MEEN?

Are there any curfew rules attached to this apartment?
Gibt es Regelungen zur Nachtruhe in dieser Wohnung?
Geebt es RAY-ge-loon-gen tsoor NAKHT-roo-he in DEE-ser VOH-noong?

How long is the lease for this place?
Wie lange gilt der Mietvertrag für diese Wohnung?
Vee LAN-ge gilt der MEET-fer-trag fuer DEE-se VOH-noong?

Do you gamble?
Spielen Sie?
SPEE-len See?

We should go to a casino.
Wir sollten ins Kasino gehen.
Veer SOLL-ten ins Ka-SEE-no GAY-hen.

There is really good horse racing in this area.
Hier gibt es ein richtig gutes Pferderennen.
Heer geebt es ighn RIKH-tig GOO-tes PFER-de-ren-nen.

Do you have your ID so that we can go gambling?
Hast du deinen Ausweis dabei, damit wir um Geld spielen können?
Hast doo DIGH-nen AUS-vighs da-BIGH, da-MIT veer um Geld SHPEE-len KOEN-nen?

Who did you bet on?
Auf wen hast du gesetzt?
Auf vayn hast doo ge-SETST?

I am calling about the apartment that you placed in the ad.
Ich rufe bezüglich der Wohnung an, für die Sie eine Anzeige geschaltet haben.
Ikh FOO-fe be-TSUEG-likh der VOH-noong an, fuer dee See IGH-ne AN-tsigh-ge ge-SHAL-tet HAH-ben.

How much did you bet?
Wie viel haben Sie gesetzt?
Vee feel HAH-ben See ge-SETST?

We should go running with the bulls!
Wir sollten zum Stierlauf gehen!
Veer SOLL-ten tsoom SHTEER-lauf GAY-hen!

Is Adele coming to sing at this venue tonight?
Wird Adele heute Abend hier singen?
Vird A-DEH-le HOY-te AH-bend heer SING-en?

How much is the item you have in the window?
Wie viel kostet der Artikel hier im Fenster?
Vee feel KOS-tet der Ar-TEE-kel heer im FEN-ster?

Do you have payment plans?
Kann man das auch auf Raten kaufen?
Kann man das aukh auf RAH-ten KAU-fen?

Do these two items come together?
Kann man diese zwei auch gemeinsam kaufen?
Kann man DEE-se tsvigh aukh ge-MIGHN-sam KAU-fen?

Are these parts cheaply made?
Sind diese Teile günstig gefertigt?
Sind DEE-se TIGH-le GUEN-stig ge-FAYR-tigt?

This is a huge bargain!
Das ist ein sehr gutes Angebot!
Das ist ighn sayr GOO-tes AN-ge-bhot!

I like this. How does three hundred dollars sound?
Das gefällt mir. Was halten Sie von dreihundert Dollar dafür?
Das ge-FAELLT meer. Vas HAL-ten See fon DRIGH-hoon-dert DOL-lar da-FUER?

Two hundred is all I can offer. That is my final price.
Zweihundert Dollar ist mein Maximum.
TSVIGH-hoon-dert DOL-lar ist mighn MAK-see-moom.

Do you have cheaper versions of this item?
Haben Sie davon auch eine günstigere Variante?
HAH-ben See DA-fon aukh IGH-ne GUENS-tee-ge-re Va-ree-AN-te?

Do you have the same item with a different pattern?
Haben Sie das auch mit einem anderen Muster?
HAH-ben See das aukh mit IGH-nem AN-de-ren MUS-ter?

How much is this worth?
Wie viel kostet das?
Vee feel KOS-tet das?

Can you pack this up and send it to my address on file?
Können Sie das einpacken und an meine schon eingespeicherte Adresse schicken?
KOEN-nen See das IGHN-pa-ken oond an MIGH-ne shohn IGHN-ge-SHPIGH-kher-te Ad-RES-se SHI-kken?

Does it fit?
Passt es?
Passt es?

They are too big for me.
Sie sind zu groß für mich.
See sind tsoo grohss fuer mikh.

Please find me another but in the same size.
Bitte suchen Sie mir nach etwas anderem in derselben Größe.
BI-te SOO-khen See meer nakh ET-vas AN-de-rem in der-SEL-ben GROE-sse.

It fits, but is tight around my waist.
Es passt, aber es ist etwas eng um meine Hüften.
Es passt, AH-ber es ist ET-was eng um MIGH-ne HUEF-ten.

Can I have one size down?
Kann ich es eine Größe kleiner haben?
Kann ikh es IGH-ne GROE-sse KLIGH-ner HAH-ben?

Size twenty, American.
Größe zwanzig, amerikanische Größe.
GROE-sse TSVAHN-tsig, a-me-ree-KAH-nee-she GROE-sse.

Do you sell appliances for the home?
Verkaufen Sie Haushaltsgeräte?
Fer-KAU-fen See HAUS-halts-ge-RAE-te?

Not now, thank you.
Nicht jetzt, danke.
NIkht yetst, DAN-ke.

I'm looking for something special.
Ich suche nach etwas Speziellem.
Ikh SOO-khe nakh ET-was Shpay-tsee-EL-lem.

I'll call you when I need you.
Ich rufe Sie, wenn ich Sie brauche.
Ikh ROO-fe See, venn ikh See BRAU-khe.

Do you have this in my size?
Haben Sie das in meiner Größe?
HAH-ben See das in migh-ner GROE-sse?

On which floor can I find cologne?
In welchem Stock finde ich Parfüm?
In VEL-khem Shtock FIN-de ikh Par-FUEM?

Where is the entrance?
Wo ist der Eingang?
Voh ist der IGHN-gang?

Do I exit from that door?
Ist dort der Ausgang?
Ist dort der AUS-gang?

Where is the elevator?
Wo ist der Lift?
Voh ist der Lift?

Do I push or pull to get this door open?
Muss ich bei der Türe drücken oder ziehen?
Muss ikh bigh der TUE-re DRUE-ken OH-der TSEE-hen?

I already have that, thanks.
Das habe ich schon, danke.
Das HAH-be ikh shohn, DAN-ke.

Where can I try this on?
Wo kann ich das anprobieren?
Voh kann ikh das AN-pro-bee-ren?

This mattress is very soft.
Diese Matratze ist sehr weich.
DEE-se Ma-TRA-tse ist sayr vighkh.

What is a good place for birthday gifts?
Wo finde ich gute Geburtstagsgeschenke?
Voh FIN-de ikh GOO-te Ge-BOORTS-tahgs-ge-SHEN-ke?

I'm just looking, but thank you.
Ich schaue mich nur um, danke.
Ikh SHAU-e mikh noor um, DAN-ke.

Yes, I will call you when I need you, thank you.
Ja, ich rufe Sie, wenn ich Sie brauche, danke.
Yah, ikh ROO-fe See, venn ikh See BRAU-khe, DAN-ke.

Do you accept returns?
Kann man das hier auch zurückgeben?
Kann man das heer aukh tsoo-RUEK-gay-ben?

Here is my card and receipt for the return.
Hier ist meine Karte und die Rechnung für die Rückgabe.
Heer ist migh-ne KAR-te oond dee REKH-noong fuer dee RUEK-gah-be.

Where are the ladies' clothes?
Wo ist die Damenbekleidung?
Voh ist dee DAH-men-be-kligh-doong?

What sizes are available for this item?
In welchen Größen haben Sie das?
In vel-khen GROE-ssen hah-ben See das?

Is there an ATM machine nearby?
Ist hier ein Geldautomat in der Nähe?
Ist heer ighn GELD-au-to-maht in der NAE-he?

What forms of payment do you accept?
Welche Zahlungsmethoden akzeptieren Sie?
VEL-khe TSAH-loongs-me-TOH-den ak-tsep-TEE-ren See?

That doesn't interest me.
Das interessiert mich nicht.
Das in-te-res-SEERT mikh nikht.

I don't like it, but thank you.
Es gefällt mir nicht, aber danke.
Es ge-FAELLT meer nikht, AH-ber DAN-ke.

Do you take American dollars?
Akzeptieren Sie amerikanische Dollar?
Ak-tsep-TEE-ren See a-me-ree-KAH-nee-she DOL-lar?

Can you make changes for me?
Können Sie das auch für mich abändern?
KOEN-nen See das aukh fuer mikh AB-aen-dern?

What is the closest place to get change for my money?
Wo kann ich hier in der Nähe Geld wechseln?
Voh kann ikh heer in der NAE-he Geld VEKH-seln?

Are travelers checks able to be changed here?
Kann ich hier Reiseschecks einlösen?
Kann ikh heer RIGH-se-sheks IGHN-loe-sen?

What is the current exchange rate?
Was sind die aktuellen Wechselkurse?
Vas sind dee ak-too-EL-len VEKH-sel-koor-se?

What is the closest place to exchange money?
Wo kann ich hier in der Nähe Geld wechseln?
Voh kann ikh heer in der NAE-he Geld VEKH-seln?

Do you need to borrow money? How much?
Willst du dir Geld leihen? Wie viel?
Villst doo deer Geld LIGH-hen? Vee feel?

Can this bank exchange my money?
Kann ich in dieser Bank mein Geld wechseln?
Kann ikh in DEE-ser Bank mighn Geld VEKH-seln?

What is the exchange rate for the American dollar?
Was ist der Wechselkurs für amerikanische Dollar?
Vas ist der VEKH-sel-koors fuer a-me-ree-KAH-nee-she DOL-lar?

Will you please exchange me fifty dollars?
Können Sie mir fünfzig Dollar wechseln?
KOEN-nen See meer FUENF-tsig DOL-lar VEKH-seln?

I would like a receipt with that.
Ich hätte gerne die Rechnung dazu.
Ikh HAE-te GAYR-ne dee REKH-noong da-TSOO.

Your commission rate is too high.
Ihr Provisionssatz ist mir zu hoch.
Eer Pro-vee-see-OHNS-sats ist meer tsoo hohhk.

Does this bank have a lower commission rate?
Hat diese Bank einen geringeren Provisionssatz?
Hat DEE-se Bank IGH-nen ge-RING-e-ren Pro-vee-see-OHNS-sats.

Do you take cash?
Akzeptieren Sie Bargeld?
Ak-tsep-TEE-ren See BAHR-geld?

Where can I exchange dollars?
Wo kann ich Dollar umwechseln?
Voh kann ikh DOL-lar UM-wekh-seln?

I want to exchange dollars for yen.
Ich möchte gerne Dollar in Yen wechseln.
Ikh MOEKH-te GAYR-ne DOL-lar in Yen VEKH-seln.

Do you take credit cards?
Akzeptieren Sie Kreditkarten?
Ak-tsep-TEE-ren See Kre-DEET-kar-ten?

Here is my credit card.
Hier ist meine Kreditkarte.
Heer ist MIGH-ne Kre-DEET-kar-te.

One moment, let me check the receipt.
Einen Moment, lassen Sie mich bitte die Rechnung überprüfen.
IGH-nen Mo-MENT, LAS-sen See mikh BI-te dee REKH-noong ue-ber-PRUE-fen.

Do I need to pay tax?
Muss ich Steuern bezahlen?
Muss ikh SHTOY-ern be-TSAH-len?

How much is this item with tax?
Was kostet das versteuert?
Vas KOS-tet das fer-STOY-ert?

Where is the cashier?
Wo ist die Kasse?
Voh ist dee KAS-se?

Excuse me, I'm looking for a dress.
Entschuldigen Sie, ich suche ein Kleid.
Ent-SHOOL-dee-gen See, ikh SOO-khe ighn Klighd.

That's a lot for that dress.
Das Kleid ist teuer.
Das Klighd ist TOY-er.

Sorry, but I don't want it.
Tut mir leid, aber ich möchte es nicht.
Toot meer Lighd, AH-ber ikh MOEKH-te es nikht.

Okay I will take it.
Okay, ich nehme es.
Oh-KAY, ikh NAY-me es.

I'm not interested if you are going to sell it at that price.
Ich habe kein Interesse zu dem Preis.
Ikh HAH-be kighn In-te-RES-se tsoo daym Prighs.

You are cheating me at the current price.
Zu dem Preis ist das Betrug.
Tsoo daym Prighs ist das Be-TROOG.

No thanks. I'll only take it if you lower the price by half.
Nein danke, ich nehme es nur zum halben Preis.
Nighn DAN-ke, ikh NAY-me es noor tsoom HAL-ben Prighs.

That is a good price, I'll take it.
Das ist ein guter Preis, ich nehme es.
Das ist ighn GOO-ter Prighs, ikh NAY-me es.

Do you sell souvenirs for tourists?
Verkaufen Sie Souvenirs für Touristen?
Fer-KAU-fen See Soo-ve-NEERS fuer Too-RIS-ten?

Can I have a bag for that?
Kann ich dafür eine Tasche haben?
Kann ikh DAH-fuer igh-ne TA-she HAH-ben?

Is this the best bookstore in the city?
Ist das der beste Buchladen in der Stadt?
Ist das der BES-te BOOKH-lah-den in der Shtat?

I would like to go to a game shop to buy comic books.
Ich würde gerne in ein Spiele-Geschäft gehen, um Comics zu kaufen.
Ikh WUER-de GAYR-ne in ighn SHPEE-le-Ge-SHAEFT GAY-hen, um KO-miks tsoo KAU-fen.

Are you able to ship my products overseas?
Können Sie das auch nach Übersee verschicken?
KOE-nen See das aukh nakh UE-ber-say fer-SHI-kken?

CHILDREN AND PETS

Which classroom does my child attend?
In welcher Klasse ist mein Kind?
In VEL-kher KLA-sse ist mighn Kind?

Is the report due before the weekend?
Muss der Bericht vor dem Wochenende fertig sein?
Muss der Be-RIKHT fohr dem VO-khen-en-de FER-tig sighn?

I'm waiting for my mom to pick me up.
Ich warte darauf, dass mich meine Mutter abholt.
Ikh VAR-te da-RAUF, dass mikh MIGH-ne MOO-tter AB-holt.

What time does the school bus run?
Wann kommt der Schulbus?
Vann kommt der SHOOL-bus?

I need to see the principal.
Ich muss den Direktor sprechen.
Ikh muss den Dee-REK-tor SHPRE-khen.

I would like to report bullying.
Ich möchte einen Fall von Mobbing melden.
Ikh MOEKH-te IGH-nen Fall fon MO-bing MEL-den.

What are the leash laws in this area?
Wie sind die Gesetze zur Leinenpflicht in dieser Gegend?
Vee sind dee Ge-SET-se tsoor LIGH-nen-pflikht in DEE-ser GAY-gend?

Please keep your dog away from mine.
Bitte halten Sie Ihren Hund von meinem fern.
BI-te HAL-ten See EE-ren Hoond fon MIGH-nem fern.

My dog doesn't bite.
Mein Hund beißt nicht.
Mighn Hoond bighsst nikht.

I am allergic to cat hair.
Ich bin allergisch auf Katzenhaare.
Ikh bin al-LER-gish auf KA-tsen-hah-re.

Don't leave the door open or the cat will run out!
Lass die Türe nicht offen, sonst läuft die Katze hinaus!
Lass dee TUE-re nikht O-ffen, sonst loyft dee KA-tse hee-NAUS!

Have you fed the dog yet?
Hast du den Hund schon gefüttert?
Hast doo den Hoond shohn ge-FUE-tert?

We need to take the dog to the veterinarian.
Wir müssen den Hund zum Tierarzt bringen.
Veer MUE-ssen den Hoond tsoom TEER-artst BRING-en.

Are there any open roster spots on the team?
Sind noch Plätze im Team frei?
Sind nokh PLAE-tse im Teem frigh?

My dog is depressed.
Mein Hund ist deprimiert.
Mighn Hoond ist de-pree-MEERT.

Don't feed the dog table scraps.
Füttere den Hund nicht vom Tisch.
FUE-te-re den Hoond nikht fom Tish.

Don't let the cat climb up on the furniture.
Lass die Katze nicht auf die Möbel hinauf.
Lass dee KA-tse nikht auf dee MOE-bel hee-NAUF.

The dog is not allowed to sleep in the bed with you.
Der Hund darf nicht mit dir im Bett schlafen.
Der Hoond darf nikht mit deer im Bett SHLAH-fen.

There is dog poop on the floor. Clean it up.
Da ist Hundekacke am Boden. Mach es sauber.
Da ist HOON-de-KA-ke am BOH-den. Makh es SAU-ber.

When was the last time you took the dog for a walk?
Wann bist du zuletzt mit dem Hund Gassi gegangen?
Vann bist doo tsoo-LETST mit dem Hoond GA-ssee ge-GAN-gen?

Are you an international student? How long are you attending?
Bist du ein Austausch-Schüler? Wie lange wirst du hier sein?
Bist doo ighn AUS-taush-SHUE-ler? Vee LAN-ge veerst doo heer sighn?

Are you a French student?
Bist du ein Austausch-Schüler aus Frankreich?
Bist doo ighn AUS-taush-SHUE-ler aus FRANK-righkh?

I am an American student that is here for the semester.
Ich bin ein Student aus den USA und für dieses Semester hier.
Ikh bin ighn Shtoo-DENT aus den OO-Es-Ah oond fuer DEE-ses Se-MES-ter heer.

Please memorize this information.
Bitte merke dir das.
BI-te MER-ke deer das.

This is my roommate Max.
Das ist mein Mitbewohner Max.
Das ist mighn MIT-be-voh-ner Maks.

Are these questions likely to appear on the exams?
Werden die Fragen auch in der Prüfung drankommen?
VER-den dee FRAH-gen aukh in der PRUE-foong DRAN-kom-men?

Teacher, say that once more, please.
Male: Können Sie das nochmal wiederholen, Herr Lehrer?
KOE-nen See das NOKH-mal vee-der-HOH-len Herr LAY-rer?
Female: Können Sie das nochmal wiederholen, Frau Lehrerin?
KOE-nen See das NOKH-mal vee-der-HOH-len Frau LAY-rer-in?

I didn't do well on the quiz.
Der Test ist nicht gut ausgefallen.
Der Test ist nikht goot AUS-ge-fal-len.

Go play outside, but stay where I can see you.
Spiel ein wenig draußen, aber bleib, wo ich dich sehen kann.
Shpeel ighn VAY-neeg DRAU-ssen, AH-ber blighb, voh ikh dikh SAY-hen kann.

How is your daughter?
Wie geht es Ihrer Tochter?
Vee gayt es EE-rer TOKH-ter?

I'm going to walk the dog.
Ich gehe mit dem Hund Gassi.
Ikh GAY-he mit dem Hoond GA-ssee.

She's not very happy here.
Sie ist nicht sehr glücklich hier.
See ist nikht sayr GLUEK-likh heer.

I passed the quiz with high marks!
Ich habe den Test mit guten Noten bestanden!
Ikh HAH-be den Test mit GOO-ten NOH-ten be-SHTAN-den!

What program are you enrolled in?
In welchem Programm bist du eingeschrieben?
In VEL-khem Pro-GRAMM bist doo IGHN-ge-shree-ben?

I really like my English teacher.
Ich mag meinen Englischlehrer wirklich.
Ikh mahg MIGH-nen ENG-lish-lehr-er VIRK-likh.

I have too much homework to do.
Ich habe zu viele Hausaufgaben auf.
Ikh HAH-be tsoo FEE-le HAUS-auf-gah-ben auf.

Tomorrow, I have to take my dog to the vet.
Morgen muss ich den Hund zum Tierarzt bringen.
MOR-gen muss ikh den Hoond tsoom TEER-artst BRIN-gen.

When do we get to go to lunch?
Wann gibt es Mittagessen?
Vann geebt es MIT-tag-es-sen?

My dog swallowed something he shouldn't have.
Mein Hund hat etwas gegessen, was er nicht hätte essen dürfen.
MIghn Hoond hat ET-vas ge-GES-sen, vas er nikht HAE-te ES-sen DUER-fen.

We need more toys for our dog to play with.
Wir brauchen mehr Spielzeug für den Hund.
Veer BRAU-khen mayr SHPEEL-tsoyg fuer den Hoond.

Can you please change the litter box?
Kannst du bitte das Katzenklo ausmisten?
Kannst doo BI-te das KA-tsen-kloh AUS-mis-ten?

118

Get a lint brush and roll it to get the hair off your clothes.
Hol dir eine Fusselbürste und entferne die Haare von deiner Kleidung.
Hohl deer IGH-ne FUSS-el-buer-ste oond ent-FER-ne dee HAH-re fon DIGH-ner KLIGH-doong.

Can you help me study?
Kannst du mir beim Lernen helfen?
Kannst doo meer bighm LER-nen HEL-fen?

I have to go study in my room.
Ich muss in meinem Zimmer lernen.
Ikh muss in MIGH-nem TSIM-mer LER-nen.

We went to the campus party, and it was a lot of fun.
Wir waren auf dem Uni-Fest und es war großartig.
Veer vah-ren auf dem U-nnee-Fest, oond es vahr GROHSS-ar-tig.

Can you use that word in a sentence?
Kannst du das Wort in einem Satz benutzen?
Kannst doo das Vort in IGH-nem Sats be-NU-tsen?

How do you spell that word?
Wie schreibt man dieses Wort?
Vee shrighbt man DEE-ses Vort?

Go play with your brother.
Spiel mit deinem Bruder.
Shpeel mit DIGH-nem BROO-der.

Come inside! It is dinnertime.
Komm herein! Es ist Essenszeit.
Komm he-RIGHN! Es ist ES-sens-tsight.

Tell me about your day.
Erzähl mir von deinem Tag.
Er-TSAEL meer fon DIGH-nem Tahg.

Is there anywhere you want to go?
Wohin magst du gehen?
VOH-hin mahgst doo GAY-hen?

How are you feeling?
Wie geht es dir?
Vee gayt es deer?

What do you want me to make for dinner tonight?
Was soll ich dir heute zum Abendessen machen?
Vas soll eekh deer HOY-te tsoom AH-bend-es-sen MA-khen?

It's time for you to take a bath.
Es ist Zeit, dass du ein Bad nimmst.
Es ist Tsight, dass doo ighn Bahd nimmst.

Brush your teeth and wash behind your ears.
Putz deine Zähne und wasch dich hinter den Ohren.
Puts DIGH-ne TSAE-ne oond vash dikh HIN-ter den OH-ren.

You're not wearing that to bed.
Das ziehst du nicht zum Schlafen an.
Das tseest doo nikht tsoom SHLAH-fen an.

I don't like the way you're dressed. Put something else on.
Mir gefällt nicht, was du anhast. Zieh etwas anderes an.
Meer ge-FAELLT nikht, vas doo AN-hast. Tsee ET-vas AN-de-res an.

Did you make any friends today?
Hast du heute neue Freunde gefunden?
Hast doo HOY-te NOY-e FROYN-de ge-FOON-den?

Let me see your homework.
Lass mich deine Hausaufgaben ansehen.
Lass mikh DIGH-ne HAUS-auf-gah-ben AN-say-hen.

Do I need to call your school?
Muss ich deine Schule anrufen?
Muss ikh DIGH-ne SHOO-le AN-roo-fen?

The dog can't go outside right now.
Der Hund kann gerade nicht rausgehen.
Der Hoond kann ge-RAH-de nikht RAUS-gay-hen.

Is the new quiz going to be available next week?
Ist der neue Test nächste Woche schon verfügbar?
Ist der NOY-e Test NAEKH-ste VO-khe shohn fer-FUEG-bar?

Are we allowed to use calculators with the test?
Dürfen wir Taschenrechner für den Test benutzen?
DUER-fen veer TA-shen-rekh-ner fuer den Test be-NOO-tsen?

I would like to lead today's lesson.
Ich möchte gerne die heutige Stunde leiten.
Ikh MOEKH-te GAYR-ne dee HOY-tee-ge SHTUN-de LIGH-ten.

I have a dorm curfew, so I need to go back.
Bei mir im Wohnheim gibt es eine Nachtruhe, ich muss zurück.
Bigh meer im VOHN-highm geebt es IGH-ne NAKHT-roo-he, ikh muss tsoo-RUEK.

Do I have to use pencil or ink?
Soll ich einen Bleistift oder einen Füller verwenden?
Soll ikh IGH-nen BLIGH-stift OH-der IGH-nen FUE-ler fer-VEN-den?

Are cell phones allowed in class?
Sind Handys im Unterricht erlaubt?
Sind HAEN-dees im UN-ter-rikht er-LAUBT?

Where can I find the nearest dog park?
Wo ist der nächste Hundepark?
Voh ist der NAEKH-ste HOON-de-park?

Are dogs allowed to be off their leash here?
Müssen Hunde hier an die Leine?
MUE-sen HOON-de heer an dee LIGH-ne?

Are children allowed here?
Sind Kinder hier erlaubt?
SIND KIN-der heer er-LAUBT?

I would like to set up a play date with our children.
Ich möchte gerne einen Spieltermin mit unseren Kindern vereinbaren.
Ikh MOEKH-te GAYR-ne IGH-nen SHPEEL-ter-meen mit UN-se-ren KIN-dern fer-IGHN-bah-ren.

I would like to invite you to my child's birthday party.
Ich möchte dich gerne zur Geburtstagsfeier meines Kindes einladen.
Ikh MOEKH-te dikh GAYR-ne tsoor Ge-BOORTS-tahgs-figh-er MIGH-nes KIN-des IGHN-lah-den.

Did you miss your dorm curfew last night?
Hast du gestern die Nachtruhe im Wohnheims verpasst?
Hast doo GES-tern DIGH-ne NAKHT-roo-he im VOHN-highm fer-PASST?

TRAVELER'S GUIDE

Over there is the library.
Die Bibliothek ist dort drüben.
Dee Bee-blee-o-TAYK ist dort DRUE-ben.

Just over there.
Da drüben.
Da DRUE-ben.

Yes, this way.
Ja, in diese Richtung.
Yah, in DEE-se RIKH-toong.

I haven't done anything wrong.
Ich habe nichts falsch gemacht.
Ikh HAH-be nikhts falsh ge-MAKHT.

It was a misunderstanding.
Das war ein Missverständnis.
Das vahr Ighn MIS-fer-staend-nis.

I am an American citizen.
Ich bin ein amerikanischer Bürger.
Ikh bin ain A-me-ree-KAH-ni-sher BUER-ger.

We are tourists on vacation.
Wir sind Touristen im Urlaub.
Veer sind Too-RIS-ten im OOR-laub.

I am looking for an apartment.
Ich suche eine Wohnung.
Ikh SOO-khe IGH-ne VOH-noong.

This is a short-term stay.
Das ist nur für eine Weile.
Das ist noor fuer IGH-ne VIGH-le.

I am looking for a place to rent.
Ich suche etwas zum Mieten.
Ikh SOO-khe ET-vas tsoom MEE-ten.

Where can we grab a quick bite to eat?
Wo können wir etwas zu essen bekommen?
Voh KOE-nen veer ET-vas tsoo ES-sen be-KOM-men?

We need the cheapest place you can find.
Wir brauchen die günstigste Bleibe, die du finden kannst.
Veer BRAU-khen dee GUEN-stig-ste BLIGH-be, dee doo FIN-den kannst.

Do you have a map of the city?
Haben Sie eine Karte der Stadt?
HAH-ben See IGH-ne KAR-te der Shtat?

What places do tourists usually visit when they come here?
Was schauen sich Touristen hier normalerweise an?
Vas SHAU-en sikh Too-RIS-sten heer nor-MAH-ler-vigh-se an?

Can you take our picture, please?
Können Sie bitte ein Foto von uns machen?
KOE-nen See BI-te ighn FOH-to fon uns MA-khen?

Do you take foreign credit cards?
Akzeptieren Sie ausländische Kreditkarten?
Ak-tsep-TEE-ren See AUS-laen-dee-she Kre-DEET-kar-ten?

I would like to hire a bicycle to take us around the city.
Ich möchte gerne ein Fahrrad ausleihen.
Ikh MOEKH-te GAYR-ne ighn FAHR-rad AUS-ligh-hen.

Do you mind if I take pictures here?
Darf ich hier Fotos machen?
Darf ikh heer FOH-tos MA-khen?

ANSWERS

Yes, to some extent.
Ja, ein bisschen.
Yah, ighn BIS-khen.

I'm not sure.
Ich bin nicht sicher.
Ikh bin nikht SI-kher.

Yes, go ahead.
Ja, machen Sie weiter.
Yah, MA-khen See VIGH-ter.

Yes, just like you.
Ja, genau wie Sie.
Yah, ge-NAU vee See.

No, no problem at all.
Nein, kein Problem.
Nighn, kighn Pro-BLAYM.

This is a little more expensive than the other item.
Das ist ein wenig teurer als das andere.
Das ist ighn VAY-nig TOY-rer als das AN-de-re.

My city is small but nice.
Meine Stadt ist klein, aber schön.
MIGH-ne Shtat ist klighn, AH-ber shoen.

This city is quite big.
Diese Stadt ist ziemlich groß.
DEE-se Shtat ist TSEEM-likh grohss.

I'm from America.
Ich bin aus den USA.
Ikh bin aus den OO-Es-AH.

We'll wait for you.
Wir warten auf dich.
Veer VAR-ten auf dikh.

I love going for walks.
Ich liebe es, spazieren zu gehen.
Ikh LEE-be es, shpa-TSEE-ren tsoo GAY-hen.

I'm a woman.
Ich bin eine Frau.
Ikh bin IGH-ne Frau.

Good, I'm going to see it.
Gut, ich werde es mir ansehen.
Goot, ikh VER-de es meer AN-say-hen.

So do I.
Ich auch.
Ikh aukh.

I'll think about it and call you tomorrow with an answer.
Ich denke darüber nach, morgen gebe ich Ihnen Bescheid.
Ikh DEN-ke da-RUE-ber nakh, MOR-gen GAY-be ikh EE-nen Be-SHIGHT.

I have two children.
Ich habe zwei Kinder.
Ikh HAH-be tsvigh KIN-der.

Does this place have a patio?
Hat es eine Terrasse?
Hat es IGH-ne Ter-RAS-se?

No, the bathroom is vacant.
Nein, das Badezimmer ist frei.
Nighn, das BAH-de-tsim-mer ist frigh.

I'm not old enough.
Ich bin noch nicht alt genug.
Ikh bin nokh nikht alt ge-NOOG.

No, it is very easy.
Nein, es ist sehr einfach.
Nighn, es ist sayr IGHN-fakh.

Understood.
Verstanden.
Fer-SHTAN-den.

Only if you go first.
Nach Ihnen.
Nakh EE-nen.

Yes, that is correct.
Ja, das stimmt.
Yah, das shtimmt.

That was the wrong answer.
Das war die falsche Antwort.
Das vahr dee FAL-she ANT-vort.

We haven't decided yet.
Wir haben es noch nicht entschieden.
Veer HAH-ben es nokh nikht ent-SHEE-den.

We can try.
Wir können es versuchen.
Veer KOE-nen es fer-SOO-khen.

I like to read books.
Ich mag es, Bücher zu lesen.
Ikh mahg es, BUE-kher tsoo LAY-sen.

We can go there together.
Wir können zusammen hingehen.
Veer KOE-nen tsoo-SAM-men Hin-gay-hen.

Yes, I see.
Ja, ich sehe es.
Yah, ikh SAY-he es.

That looks interesting.
Das sieht interessant aus.
Das seet in-te-res-SANT aus.

Me neither.
Ich auch nicht.
Ikh aukh nikht.

It was fun.
Es war lustig.
Es vahr LOOS-tig.

Me too.
Mir auch.
Meer aukh.

Stay there.
Bleib hier.
Blighb heer.

We were worried about you.
Wir haben uns Sorgen um dich gemacht.
Veer HAH-ben uns SOR-gen um dikh ge-MAKHT.

No, not really.
Nein, nicht wirklich.
Nighn, nikht VEERK-likh.

Unbelievable.
Unglaublich.
Un-GLAUB-likh.

No, I didn't make it in time.
Nein, ich habe es nicht rechtzeitig geschafft.
Nighn, ikh HAH-be es nikht REKHT-tsai-tig ge-SHAFFT.

No, you cannot.
Nein, kannst du nicht.
Nighn, kannst doo nikht.

Here you go.
Los geht's.
Lohs gayts.

It was good.
Es war gut.
Es vahr goot.

Ask my wife.
Fragen Sie meine Frau.
FRAH-gen See MIGH-ne Frau.

That's up to him.
Das soll er entscheiden.
Das soll ayr ent-SHIGH-den.

That is not allowed.
Das ist verboten.
Das ist fer-BOH-ten.

You can stay at my place.
Du kannst bei mir bleiben.
Doo kannst bigh meer BLIGH-ben.

Only if you want to.
Nur, wenn du willst.
Noor, venn doo villst.

It depends on my schedule.
Es hängt von meinem Zeitplan ab.
Es haengt fon MIGH-nem TSIGHT-plahn ab.

I don't think that's possible.
Ich glaube, das wird nicht möglich sein.
Ikh GLAU-be, das vird nikht MOE-glikh sighn.

You're not bothering me.
Sie stören mich nicht.
See SHTOE-ren mikh nikht.

The salesman will know.
Der Verkäufer wird es wissen.
Der Fer-KOY-fer vird es VI-ssen.

I have to work.
Ich muss arbeiten.
Ikh muss AR-bigh-ten.

I'm late.
Ich bin zu spät.
Ikh bin tsoo shpaet.

To pray.
Um zu beten.
Um tsoo BAY-ten.

I'll do my best.
Ich gebe mein Bestes.
Ikh GAY-be mighn BES-tes.

DIRECTIONS

Over here.
Hierher.
HEER-hayr.

Go straight ahead.
Gehen Sie geradeaus.
GAY-hen See ge-RAH-de-aus.

Follow the straight line.
Folgen Sie der geraden Linie.
FOL-gen See der ge-RAH-den LEE-nee-e.

Go halfway around the circle.
Gehen Sie zur Hälfte um den Kreis.
GAY-hen See tsoor HAELF-te um den Krighs.

It is to the left.
Es ist zu Ihrer linken Seite.
Es ist tsoo EE-rer LIN-ken SIGH-te.

Where is the party going to be?
Wo wird die Party stattfinden?
Voh vird dee Par-tee SHTAT-fin-den?

Where is the library situated?
Wo ist die Bibliothek?
Voh ist dee Bee-blee-o-TAYK?

It is to the north.
Es ist in Richtung Norden.
Es ist in RIKH-toong NOR-den.

You can find it down the street.
Sie können es weiter unten auf dieser Straße finden.
See KOE-nen es VIGH-ter UN-ten auf DEE-ser SHTRAH-sse FIN-den.

Go into the city to get there.
Gehen Sie in die Stadt, um dorthin zu gelangen.
GAY-hen See in dee Shtat, um DORT-hin tsoo ge-LAN-gen.

Where are you now?
Wo sind Sie jetzt?
Voh sind See yetst?

There is a fire hydrant right in front of me.
Direkt vor mir ist ein Hydrant.
Dee-REKT fohr meer ist ighn Hue-DRANT.

Do you know a shortcut?
Kennen Sie eine Abkürzung?
KEN-nen See IGH-ne AB-kuer-tsoong?

Where is the freeway?
Wo ist die Autobahn?
Voh ist dee AU-to-baan?

Do I need exact change for the toll?
Muss ich die Maut genau bezahlen?
Muss ikh dee Maut ge-NAU be-TSAH-len?

At the traffic light, turn right.
An der Ampel biegen Sie rechts ab.
An der AM-pel BEE-gen See rekhts ab.

When you get to the intersection, turn left.
An der Kreuzung biegen Sie links ab.
An der KROY-tsoong BEE-gen See links ab.

Stay in your lane until it splits off to the right.
Bleiben Sie auf der Spur, bis Sie nach rechts abbiegen können.
BLIGH-ben See auf der Shpoor, bis See nach rekhts AB-bee-gen KOE-nen.

Don't go onto the ramp.
Nicht die Rampe hinauffahren.
NIkht dee RAM-pe hee-NAUF-fah-ren.

You are going in the wrong direction.
Wir sind falsch unterwegs.
Veer sind falsh un-ter-VAYGS.

Can you guide me to this location?
Können Sie mir den Weg dorthin erklären?
KOE-nen See meer den Vayg DORT-hin er-KLAE-ren?

Stop at the crossroads.
Halten Sie an der Kreuzung.
HAL-ten See an der KROY-tsoong.

You missed our turn. Please turn around.
Sie haben die Abzweigung verpasst. Bitte kehren Sie um.
See HAH-ben dee AB-tsvigh-goong fer-PASST. BI-te KAY-ren See um.

It is illegal to turn here.
Es ist verboten, hier umzukehren.
Es ist fer-BOH-ten, heer UM-tsoo-kay-ren.

We're lost, could you help us?
Wir haben uns verlaufen, können Sie uns helfen?
Veer HAH-ben uns fer-LAU-fen, KOE-nen See uns HEL-fen?

APOLOGIES

Dad, I'm sorry.
Es tut mir leid, Papa.
Es toot meer lighd, PA-pa.

I apologize for being late.
Entschuldige, dass ich zu spät bin.
Ent-SHOOL-dee-ge, dass ikh tsoo shpaet bin.

Excuse me for not bringing money.
Entschuldige, dass ich kein Geld mithabe.
Ent-SHOOL-dee-ge, dass ikh kighn Geld MIT-hah-be.

That was my fault.
Das war meine Schuld.
Das vahr MIGH-ne Shuld.

It won't happen again, I'm sorry.
Das tut mir leid, es wird nicht wieder passieren.
Das toot meer lighd, es vird nikht VEE-der pas-SEE-ren.

I won't break another promise.
Ich werde meine Versprechen in Zukunft halten.
Ikh VAYR-de MIGH-ne Fer-SHPRE-khen in TSOO-kunft HAL-ten.

You have my word that I'll be careful.
Ich verspreche, vorsichtig zu sein.
Ikh fer-SHPRE-khe, FOHR-sikh-tig tsoo sighn.

I'm sorry, I wasn't paying attention.
Tut mir leid, ich habe nicht aufgepasst.
Toot meer lighd, ikh HAH-be nikht AUF-ge-passt.

I regret that. I'm so sorry.
Ich bereue es. Es tut mir so leid.
Ikh be-ROY-e es. Es toot meer soh lighd.

I'm sorry, but today I can't.

Es tut mir leid, aber heute kann ich nicht.

Es toot meer lighd, AH-ber HOY-te kann ikh nikht.

It's not your fault, I'm sorry.

Es ist nicht deine Schuld, es tut mir leid.

Es ist nikht DIGH-ne Shuld, es toot meer lighd.

Please, give me another chance.

Bitte gib mir noch eine Chance.

BI-te geeb meer nokh IGH-ne Shaws.

Will you ever forgive me?

Wirst du mir jemals vergeben?

Virst doo meer yay-mahls fer-gay-ben?

I hope in time we can still be friends.

Ich hoffe, wir können wieder Freunde sein.

Ikh HOF-fe, veer KOE-nen VEE-der FROYN-de sighn.

I screwed up, and I'm sorry.

Ich habe versagt, tut mir leid.

Ikh HAH-be fer-SAHGT, toot meer lighd.

SMALL TALK

No.
Nein.
Nighn.

Yes.
Ja.
Yah.

Okay.
Okay.
Oh-KAY.

Please.
Bitte.
BI-te.

Do you fly out of the country often?
Verreisen Sie öfter?
Fer-RIGH-sen See OEF-ter?

Thank you.
Danke.
DAN-ke.

That's okay.
Kein Problem.
Kighn Pro-BLAYM.

I went shopping.
Ich bin einkaufen gegangen.
Ikh bin IGHN-kau-fen ge-GAN-gen.

There.
Tada.
Ta-DAH.

Very well.
Sehr gut.
Sayr goot.

What?
Wie bitte?
VEE BI-te?

I think you'll like it.
Ich glaube, du wirst es mögen.
Ikh GLAU-be, doo virst es MOE-gen.

When?
Wann?
Vann?

I didn't sleep well.
Ich habe nicht gut geschlafen.
Ikh HAH-be nikht goot ge-SHLAH-fen.

Until what time?
Bis wann?
Bis vann?

We are waiting in line.
Wir warten in der Schlange.
Veer VAHR-ten in der SHLAN-ge.

We're only waiting for a little bit longer.
Wir warten nur noch ein bisschen.
Veer VAHR-ten noor nokh ighn BIS-khen.

How?
Wie?
Vee?

Where?
Wo?
Voh?

I'm glad.
Ich bin froh.
Ikh bin froh.

You are very tall.
Sie sind sehr groß.
See sind sayr grohss.

I like to speak your language.
Ich mag es, Ihre Sprache zu sprechen.
Ikh mahg es, EE-re SHPAH-khe tsoo SHPRAY-khen.

You are very kind.
Sie sind sehr freundlich.
See sind sayr FROYND-likh.

Happy birthday!
Herzlichen Glückwunsch zum Geburtstag!
HERTS-likh-en GLUEKK-voonsh tsoom Ge-BOORTS-tahg!

I would like to thank you very much.
Ich möchte Ihnen danken.
Ikh MOEKH-te EE-nen DAN-ken.

Here is a gift that I bought for you.
Hier ist ein Geschenk für Sie.
Heer ist ighn Ge-SHENK fuer See.

Yes. Thank you for all of your help.
Ja. Danke für Ihre Hilfe.
Yah. DAN-ke fuer EE-re HIL-fe.

What did you get?
Was haben Sie bekommen?
Vas HAH-ben See be-KOM-men?

Have a good trip!
Gute Reise!
GOO-te RIGH-se!

This place is very special to me.
Das ist ein besonderer Ort für mich.
Das ist ighn be-SON-der-er Ort fuer mikh.

My foot is asleep.
Mein Fuß ist eingeschlafen.
Mighn Fooss ist IGHN-ge-shlah-fen.

May I open this now or later?
Kann ich es jetzt öffnen oder später?
Kann ikh es yetst OEFF-nen OH-der SHPAE-ter?

Why do you think that is?
Warum, glauben Sie, ist das so?
Va-ROOM, GLAU-ben See, ist das so?

Which do you like better, chocolate or caramel?
Was mögen Sie lieber, Schokolade oder Karamell?
Vas MOE-gen See LEE-ber, Shoh-koh-LAH-de OH-der Ka-ra-MELL?

Be safe on your journey.
Passen Sie auf sich auf.
PAS-sen See auf sikh auf.

I want to do this for a little longer.
Ich möchte das noch ein wenig länger machen.
Ikh MOEKH-te das nokh ighn VAY-nig LAEN-ger MA-khen.

This is a picture that I took at the hotel.
Dieses Bild habe ich im Hotel gemacht.
DEE-ses Bild HAH-be ikh im Ho-TEL ge-MAKHT.

Allow me.
Sie erlauben?
See er-LAU-ben?

I was surprised.
Ich bin überrascht.
Ikh bin ue-ber-RASHT.

I like that.
Ich mag das.
Ikh mahg das.

Are you in high spirits today?
Sind Sie heute gut gelaunt?
Sind See HOY-te goot ge-LAUNT?

Oh, here comes my wife.
Ah, hier kommt meine Frau.
Ah, heer kommt MIGH-ne Frau.

Can I see the photograph?
Darf ich das Foto sehen?
Darf ikh das FOH-to SAY-hen?

Feel free to ask me anything.
Sie dürfen mich alles fragen.
See DUER-fen mikh AL-les FRAH-gen.

That was magnificent!
Das war wunderschön!
Das wahr VONN-der-shoen!

See you some other time.
Wir sehen uns!
Veer SAY-hen uns!

No more, please.
Nicht mehr, bitte.
Nikht mayr, BI-te

Please don't use that.
Bitte verwenden Sie das nicht.
BI-te fer-VENN-den See das nikht.

That is very pretty.
Das eest sehr schön.
Das eest sehr shoen.

Would you say that again?
Würden Sie das noch einmal wiederholen?
VUER-den See das nokh IGHN-mal vee-der-HOH-len?

Speak slowly.
Sprechen Sie langsam.
SHPRAY-khen See LANG-sahm.

I'm home.
Ich bin zuhause.
Ikh bin tsoo-HAU-se.

Is this your home?
Ist das Ihr Zuhause?
Ist das Eer Tsoo-HAU-se?

I know a lot about the area.
Ich kenne die Gegend gut.
Ikh KEN-ne dee GAY-gend goot.

Welcome back. How was your day?
Willkommen zurück. Wie war Ihr Tag?
Vill-KOM-men tsoo-RUEK. Vee vahr Eer Tahg?

I read every day.
Ich lese jeden Tag.
Ikh LAY-se YAY-den Tahg.

My favorite type of book is novels by Stephen King.
Meine Lieblingsbücher sind die von Stephen King.
MIGH-ne LEEB-lings-bue-kher sind dee fon STEE-fen King.

You surprised me!
Sie überraschen mich!
See ue-ber-RAH-shen mikh!

I am short on time, so I have to go.
Ich habe keine Zeit, darum muss ich gehen.
Ikh HAH-be KIGH-ne Tsight, DAH-rum muss ikh GAY-hen.

Thank you for having this conversation.
Danke für das Gespräch.
DAN-ke fuer das GAY-shpraekh.

Oh, when is it?
Oh, wann ist es?
Oh, vann ist ays?

This is my brother, Jeremy.
Das ist mein Bruder, Jeremy.
Das ist mighn BROO-der, TSHE-re-mee.

That is my favorite bookstore.
Das ist mein Lieblings-Buchladen.
Das ist mighn LEEB-lings-Bukh-lah-den.

That statue is bigger than it looks.
Diese Statue ist größer, als sie aussieht.
DEE-se SHTAH-too-e ist GROE-sser als see AUS-seet.

Look at the shape of that cloud!

Schau dir die Form dieser Wolke an!

Shau deer dee Form DEE-ser VOL-ke an!

BUSINESS

I am president of the credit union.
Ich bin der Vorsitzende der Kreditgenossenschaft.
Ikh bin der FOHR-si-tsen-de der Kre-DEET-ge-nos-sen-shaft.

We are expanding in your area.
Wir erweitern unser Geschäft in Ihrer Gegend.
Veer er-VIGH-tern UN-ser Ge-SHAEFT in EE-rer GAY-gend.

I am looking for work in the agriculture field.
Ich suche Arbeit in der Landwirtschaft.
Ikh SOO-khe AR-bight in dayr LAND-virt-shaft.

Sign here, please.
Bitte unterschreiben Sie hier.
BI-te un-ter-SHRIGH-ben See heer.

I am looking for temporary work.
Ich suche Arbeit auf Zeit.
Ikh SOO-khe AR-bight auf Tsight.

I need to call and set up that meeting.
Ich muss anrufen und das Treffen arrangieren.
Ikh muss AN-roo-fen oond das TRE-fen ah-rang-SHEE-ren.

Is the line open?
Ist die Leitung frei?
Ist dee LIGH-toong frigh?

I need you to hang up the phone.
Sie müssen das Gespräch beenden.
See MUE-ssen das Ge-SHPRAEKH be-EN-den.

Who should I ask for more information about your business?
Wen kann ich für mehr Informationen über Ihr Unternehmen befragen?
Vayn kann ikh fuer mayr In-for-ma-tsee-OH-nen UE-ber Eer Un-ter-NAY-men be-FRAH-gen?

There was no answer when you handed me the phone.
Da war niemand dran, als Sie mir das Telefon übergeben haben.
Da vahr NEE-mand dran, als See meer das TE-le-fon ue-ber-GAY-ben HAH-ben.

Robert is not here at the moment.
Robert ist gerade nicht da.
ROH-bert ist ge-RAH-de nikht dah.

Call me after work, thanks.
Rufen Sie mich nach der Arbeit an, danke.
ROO-fen See mikh nakh der AR-bight an, DAN-ke.

We're strongly considering your contract offer.
Wir sind sehr angetan von Ihrem Angebot.
Veer sind sayr AN-ge-tahn fon EE-rem AN-ge-boht.

Have the necessary forms been signed yet?
Sind die notwendigen Formulare bereits ausgefüllt?
Sind dee NOHT-ven-dee-gen For-moo-LAH-re be-RIGHTS AUS-ge-fuellt?

I have a few hours available after work.
Ich habe nach der Arbeit ein paar Stunden frei.
Ikh HAH-be nakh der AR-bight ighn paar SHTUN-den frigh.

What do they make there?
Was machen die hier?
Vas MA-khen dee heer?

I have no tasks assigned to me.
Ich habe keine Aufgaben zugeteilt bekommen.
Ikh HAH-be KIGH-ne AUF-gah-ben TSOO-ge-tighlt be-KOM-men.

How many workers are they hiring?
Wie viele Leute stellen die ein?
Vee FEE-le LOY-te SHTE-len dee ighn?

It should take me three hours to complete this task.
Ich sollte dafür drei Stunden brauchen.
Ikh SOLL-te DAH-fuer drigh SHTUN-den BRAU-khen.

Don't use that computer, it is only for financial work.
Bitte verwenden Sie den Computer nicht, der ist nur für Finanzielles gedacht.

BI-te fer-VEN-den See den Komp-YOO-ter nikht, der ist noor fuer Fee-nan-tsee-EL-les ge-DAKHT.

I only employ people that I can rely on.
Ich stelle nur Leute ein, auf die ich mich verlassen kann.
Ikh SHTE-le noor LOY-te ighn, auf dee ikh mikh fer-LA-ssen kann.

After I talk to my lawyers, we can discuss this further.
Wir führen das fort, sobald ich mit meinen Anwälten gesprochen habe.
Veer FUE-ren das fort, so-BALD ikh mit MIGH-nen AN-vael-ten ge-SHPRO-khen HAH-be.

Are there any open positions in my field?
Gibt es noch Job-Angebote in meinem Bereich?
Geebt es nokh TSHOB-An-ge-boh-te in MIGH-nem Be-RIGHKH?

I'll meet you in the conference room.
Wir sehen uns im Konferenzzimmer.
Veer SAY-hen uns im Kon-fe-RENTS-tsim-mer.

Call and leave a message on my office phone.
Hinterlassen Sie mir eine Nachricht auf meinem Geschäftstelefon.
Hin-ter-LAS-sen See meer IGH-ne NAHKH-rikht auf MIGH-nem Ge-SHAEFTS-te-le-fohn.

Send me a fax with that information.
Schicken Sie mir ein Fax mit diesen Informationen.
SHI-ken See meer ighn Faks mit DEE-sen In-for-ma-tsee-OH-nen.

Hi, I would like to leave a message for Sheila.
Hallo, ich würde gerne eine Nachricht für Sheila hinterlassen.
HA-lo, ikh VUER-de GAYR-ne IGH-ne NAHKH-rikht fuer SHEE-la hin-ter-LAS-sen.

Please repeat your last name.
Können Sie Ihren Nachnamen bitte nochmal wiederholen?
KOE-nen See EE-ren NAHKH-nah-men BI-te NOKH-mahl vee-der-HOH-len?

I would like to buy wholesale.
Ich würde gerne einen Großhandelseinkauf machen.
Ikh VUER-de GAYR-ne IGH-nen GROHSS-han-dels-ighn-kauf MA-khen.

How do you spell your last name?
Wie schreibt man Ihren Nachnamen?
Vee shrighbt man EE-ren NAHKH-nah-men?

I called your boss yesterday and left a message.
Ich habe Ihrem Chef gestern eine Nachricht hinterlassen.
Ikh HAH-be EE-rem Shef GES-tern IGH-ne NAHKH-rikht hin-ter-LAS-sen.

That customer hung up on me.
Dieser Kunde hat einfach aufgelegt.
DEE-ser KUN-de hat IGHN-fakh AUF-ge-legt.

She called but didn't leave a callback number.
Sie hat angerufen, aber keine Nummer für den Rückruf hinterlassen.
See hat AN-ge-roo-fen, AH-ber KIGH-ne NUM-mer fuer den RUEK-roof hin-ter-LAS-sen.

Hello! Am I speaking to Bob?
Hallo! Spreche ich mit Bob?
HA-lo! SHPRAY-khe ikh mit Bob?

Excuse me, but could you speak up? I can't hear you.
Entschuldigen Sie, aber können Sie lauter sprechen? Ich kann Sie nicht verstehen.
Ent-SHOOL-dee-gen See, AH-ber KOE-nen See LAU-ter SHPRAY-khen? Ikh kann See nikht fer-SHTAY-hen.

The line is very bad, could you move to a different area so I can hear you better?
Die Verbindung ist sehr schlecht, können Sie woanders hingehen, damit ich Sie besser hören kann?
Dee Fer-BIN-doong ist sayr shlekht, KOE-nen See voh-AN-ders HIN-gay-hen, da-MIT ikh See BE-ser HOE-ren kann?

I would like to apply for a work visa.
Ich möchte gerne ein Arbeitsvisum beantragen.
Ikh MOEKH-te GAYR-ne ighn AR-bights-vee-soom be-AN-trah-gen.

It is my dream to work here teaching the language.
Es ist mein Traum, hier als Sprachlehrer zu arbeiten.
Es ist mighn Traum, heer als SHPRAHKH-lay-rer tsoo AR-bigh-ten.

I have always wanted to work here.
Ich wollte immer schon hier arbeiten.
Ikh VOLL-te IM-mer shohn heer AR-bigh-ten.

Where do you work?
Wo arbeiten Sie?
Voh AR-bigh-ten See?

Are we in the same field of work?
Arbeiten wir in der gleichen Branche?
AR-bigh-ten veer in der GLIGH-khen BRAW-she?

Do we share an office?
Sind wir im selben Büro?
Sind veer im SEL-ben Bue-ROH?

What do you do for a living?
Was arbeiten Sie?
Vas AR-bigh-ten See?

I work in the city as an engineer for Cosco.
Ich arbeite in der Stadt als Ingenieur für Cosco.
Ikh AR-bigh-te in der Shtat als In-she-nee-OER fuer KOS-koh.

I am an elementary teacher.
Ich bin Grundschullehrer.
Ikh bin GROOND-shool-layr-er.

What time should I be at the meeting?
Wann sollte ich am Treffpunkt sein?
Vann SOLL-te ikh am TREFF-punkt sighn?

Would you like me to catch you up on what the meeting was about?
Wollen Sie, dass ich Sie auf den laufenden Stand über das Meeting
bringe?
VOL-len See, dass ikh See auf den LAU-fen-den Shtand UE-ber das MEE-ting BRING-e?

I would like to set up a meeting with your company.
Ich möchte gerne ein Meeting mit Ihrem Unternehmen arrangieren.
Ikh MOEKH-te GAYR-ne ighn MEE-ting mit EE-rem Un-ter-NAY-men ar-rong-SHEE-ren.

Please, call my secretary for that information.
Bitte fragen Sie meine Sekretärin danach.
BI-te FRAH-gen See MIGH-ne Se-kre-TAE-rin da-NAKH.

I will have to ask my lawyer.
Dazu muss ich meinen Anwalt fragen.
DAH-tsoo muss ikh MIGH-nen AN-walt FRAH-gen.

Fax it over to my office number.
Faxen Sie es an meine Geschäftsnummer.
FAK-sen See es an MIGH-ne Ge-SHAEFTS-num-mer.

Will I have any trouble calling into the office?
Wird es problematisch sein, das Büro zu erreichen?
Vird es pro-blay-MAH-tish sighn, das Bue-ROH tsoo er-RIGH-khen?

Do you have a business card I can have?
Haben Sie eine Visitenkarte für mich?
HAH-ben See IGH-ne Vee-SEE-ten-kar-te fuer mikh?

Here is my business card. Please, take it.
Hier ist meine Visitenkarte für Sie.
Heer ist MIGH-ne Vee-SEE-ten-kar-te fuer See.

My colleague and I are going to lunch.
Mein Kollege und ich gehen gemeinsam Mittagessen.
Mighn Kol-LAY-ge oond ikh GAY-hen ge-MIGHN-sam MIT-tahg-es-sen.

I am the director of finance for my company.
Ich bin Finanzdirektor meines Unternehmens.
Ikh bin Fee-NANTS-dee-rek-tohr MIGH-nes Un-ter-NAY-mens.

I manage the import goods of my company.
Ich bin in meinem Unternehmen für Importe zuständig.
Ikh bin in MIGH-nem Un-ter-NAY-men fuer Im-POR-te TSOO-shtaen-dig.

My colleagues' boss is Steven.
Der Chef meines Kollegen heißt Steven.
Der Shef MIGH-nes Kol-LAY-gen highsst STEE-ven.

I work for the gas station company.
Ich arbeite für das Tankstellen-Unternehmen.
Ikh AR-bigh-te fuer das TANK-shtel-len-Un-ter-nay-men.

What company do you work for?
In welchem Unternehmen arbeiten Sie?
In VEL-khem Un-ter-NAY-men AR-bigh-ten See?

I'm an independent contractor.
Ich bin Freiberufler.
Ikh bin FRIGH-be-roof-ler.

How many employees do you have at your company?
Wie viele Mitarbeiter hat Ihr Unternehmen?
Vee FEE-le MIT-ar-bigh-ter hat Eer Un-ter-NAY-men?

I know a lot about engineering.
Ich weiß viel über Technik.
Ikh vighss feel UE-ber TEKH-nik.

I can definitely resolve that dispute for you.
Ich kann Ihnen helfen, den Konflikt zu lösen.
Ikh kann EE-nen HEL-fen, den Kon-FLIKT tsoo LOE-sen.

You should hire an interpreter.
Sie sollten einen Dolmetscher einstellen.
See SOLL-ten IGH-nen DOL-met-sher IGHN-shtel-len.

Are you hiring any additional workers?
Stellen Sie zusätzliche Mitarbeiter ein?
SHTEL-len See TSOO-saets-lee-khe MIT-ar-bigh-ter ighn?

How much experience do I need to work here?
Wie viel Erfahrung braucht man, um hier arbeiten zu dürfen?
Vee feel Er-FAH-roong braukht man, um heer AR-bigh-ten tsoo DUER-fen?

Our marketing manager handles that.
Unser Marketing-Manager kümmert sich darum.
UN-ser MAR-ke-ting-Mae-nae-dsher KUE-mert sikh dah-RUM.

I would like to poach one of your workers.
Ich möchte gerne einen Ihrer Angestellten abwerben.
Ikh MOEKH-te GAYR-ne IGH-nen EE-rer AN-ge-shtell-ten AB-ver-ben.

Can we work out a deal that is beneficial for the both of us?
Können wir einen Win-Win-Deal finden?
KOE-nen veer IGH-nen Win-Win-Deel FIN-den?

My resources are at your disposal.
Meine Ressourcen stehen Ihnen zur Verfügung.
MIGH-ne Re-SOOR-sen SHTAY-hen EE-nen tsoor Fer-FUE-goong.

I am afraid that we have to let you go.
Wir müssen Ihnen leider kündigen.
Veer MUE-sen EE-nen LIGH-der KUEN-dee-gen.

This is your first warning. Please don't do that again.
Dies ist Ihre erste Warnung. Bitte machen Sie das nicht noch einmal.
Dees ist EE-re AYR-ste VAR-noong. BI-te MA-khen See das nikht nokh IGHN-mal.

File a complaint with HR about the incident.
Melden Sie den Vorfall in der Personalabteilung.
MEL-den See den FOR-fall in der Per-so-NAHL-ab-TIGH-loong.

Who is showing up for our lunch meeting?
Wer kommt zu unserem Treffen zum Mittagessen?
Vehr kommt tsoo UN-se-rem TRE-fen tsoom MIT-tahg es-sen?

Clear out the rest of my day.
Machen Sie mir den Rest meines Tages frei.
MA-khen See meer dayn Rest MIGH-nes TAH-ges frigh.

We need to deposit this into the bank.
Wir müssen das auf die Bank bringen.
Veer MUE-sen das auf dee Bank BRING-en.

Can you cover the next hour for me?
Können Sie mich für die nächste Stunde vertreten?
KOE-nen See mikh fuer dee NAEKHS-te SHTUN-de fer-TRAY-ten?

If Shania calls, please push her directly through.
Wenn Shania anruft, stellen Sie sie direkt zu mir durch.
Venn Sha-ni-a AN-rooft, SHTEL-len See see dee-REKT tsoo meer durkh.

I'm leaving early today.
Ich gehe heute früher.
Ikh GAY-he HOY-te FRUE-her.

I'll be working late tonight.
Ich werde heute bis spät abends arbeiten.
Ikh VER-de HOY-te bis spaet AH-bends AR-bigh-ten.

You can use the bathroom in my office.
Sie können das Klo in meinem Büro benutzen.
See KOE-nen das Kloh in MIGH-nem Bue-ROH be-NU-tsen.

You can use my office phone to call out.
Sie können mein Bürotelefon benutzen.
See KOE-nen mighn Bue-ROH-te-le-fohn be-NU-tsen.

Please, close the door behind you.
Bitte schließen Sie die Türe hinter sich.
BI-te SHLEE-ssen See dee TUE-re HIN-ter sikh.

I need to talk to you privately.
Ich muss vertraulich mit Ihnen sprechen.
Ikh muss fer-TRAU-likh mit EE-nen SHPRAY-khen.

Your team is doing good work on this project.
Ihr Team leistet gute Arbeit für das Projekt.
Eer Teem LIGHS-tet GOO-te AR-bight fuer das Proh-YEKT.

Our numbers are down this quarter.
Unsere Zahlen sind schlecht in diesem Quartal.
Un-se-re TSAH-len sind shlekht in DEE-sem Kvar-TAHL.

I need you to work harder than usual.
Sie müssen nun härter als sonst arbeiten.
See MUE-sen noon HAER-ter als sonst AR-bigh-ten.

I'm calling in sick today. Can anyone cover my shift?
Ich bin heute krank. Kann mich jemand vertreten?
Ikh bin HOY-te krank. Kann mikh YAY-mand fer-TRAY-ten?

Tom, we are thinking of promoting you.
Tom, wir denken darüber nach, Sie zu befördern.
Tom, veer DEN-ken da-RUE-ber nakh, See tsoo be-FOER-dern.

I would like a raise.
Ich möchte gerne eine Gehaltserhöhung.
Ikh MOEKH-te GAYR-ne IGH-ne Ge-HALTS-er-HOE-oong.

THE WEATHER

I think the weather is changing.
Ich glaube, das Wetter wird umschlagen.
Ikh GLAU-be, das VET-ter veerd UM-shlah-gen.

Be careful, it is raining outside.
Achtung, es regnet draußen.
AKH-toong, es RAY-gnet DRAU-ssen.

Make sure to bring your umbrella
Denken Sie an Ihren Regenschirm.
DEN-ken See an EE-ren RAY-gen-shirm.

Get out of the rain or you will catch a cold.
Gehen Sie aus dem Regen, sonst werden Sie noch krank.
GAY-hen See aus daym RAY-gen, sonst VAYR-den See nokh krank.

Is it snowing?
Schneit es?
Shnight es?

The snow is very thick right now.
Es liegt derzeit viel Schnee.
Es leegt DAYR-tsight feel Shnay.

Be careful, the road is full of ice.
Achtung, die Straßen sind vereist.
AKH-toong, dee SHTRAH-ssen sind fer-IGHST.

What is the climate like here? Is it warm or cold?
Wie ist das Wetter bei Ihnen? Ist es warm oder kalt?
Vee ist das VET-ter bigh EE-nen? Ist es vahrm OH-der kalt?

It has been a very nice temperature here.
Es war sehr warm hier.
Es vahr sayr vahrm heer.

Does it rain a lot here?
Regnet es dort viel?
RAY-gnet es dort feel?

The temperature is going to break records this week.
Es wird diese Woche noch Rekord-Temperaturen geben.
Es vird DEE-se VO-khe nokh Re-KORD-Tem-pe-ra-TOO-ren GAY-ben.

Does it ever snow here?
Schneit es hier nie?
Shnight es heer nee?

When does it get sunny?
Wann wird es sonnig?
Vann vird es SO-nnig?

What's the forecast look like for tomorrow?
Wie wird das Wetter morgen?
Vee vird das VET-ter MOR-gen?

This is a heatwave.
Das ist eine Hitzewelle.
Das ist IGH-ne HI-tse-vel-le.

Right now, it is overcast, but it should clear up by this evening.
Jetzt gerade ist es bewölkt, aber abends sollte es etwas aufklaren.
Yetst ge-RAH-de ist es be-VOELKT, AH-ber AH-bends SOLL-te es ET-vas AUF-klah-ren.

It is going to heat up in the afternoon.
Wird es am Nachmittag heißer werden?
VIRD es am NAKH-mi-tahg HIGH-sser VAYR-den?

What channel is the weather channel?
Welcher Sender ist der Wetterkanal?
VEL-kher SEN-der ist dayr VET-ter-ka-nahl?

Tonight it will be below freezing.
Heute Nacht wird es Frost geben.
HOY-te Nakht vird es Frost GAY-ben.

It's very windy outside.
Es ist sehr windig draußen.
Es ist sayr VIN-dig DRAU-ssen.

It's going to be cold in the morning.
Es wird kalt am Morgen.
Es vird kalt am MOR-gen.

It's not raining, only drizzling.
Es regnet nicht, es nieselt nur.
Es RAY-gnet nikht, es NEE-selt noor.

HOTEL

I would like to book a room.
Ich möchte bitte ein Zimmer buchen.
Ikh MOEKH-te BI-te ighn TSI-mer BOO-khen.

I'd like a single room.
Ich möchte bitte ein Einzelzimmer.
Ikh MOEKH-te BI-te ighn IGHN-tsel-tsi-mer.

I'd like a suite.
Ich möchte eine Suite.
Ikh MOEKH-te IGH-ne Suite.

How much is the room per night?
Was kostet das Zimmer pro Nacht?
Vas KOS-tet das TSI-mer proh Nakht?

How much is the room with tax?
Was kostet das Zimmer inklusive Steuern?
Vas KOS-tet das TSI-mer IN-kloo-see-fe SHTOY-ern?

When is the checkout time?
Wann muss ich auschecken?
Vann muss ikh AUS-tshe-ken?

I'd like a room with a nice view.
Ich möchte gerne ein Zimmer mit schöner Aussicht.
Ikh MOEKH-te GAYR-ne ighn TSI-mer mit SHOE-ner AUS-sikht.

I'd like to order room service.
Ich möchte gerne den Zimmerservice bestellen.
Ikh MOEKH-te GAYR-ne dayn TSI-mer-ser-vis be-SHTEL-len.

Let's go swim in the outdoor pool.
Lass uns im Außenpool schwimmen gehen.
Lass uns im AU-ssen-pool SHVIM-men GAY-hen.

Are pets allowed at the hotel?
Sind Haustiere im Hotel erlaubt?
Sind HAUS-tee-re im Ho-TEL er-LAUBT?

I would like a room on the first floor.
Ich möchte gerne ein Zimmer im ersten Stock.
Ikh MOEKH-te GAYR-ne ighn TSI-mer im AYR-sten Shtok.

Can you send maintenance up to our room for a repair?
Können Sie jemanden für Reparaturen aufs Zimmer schicken?
KOE-nen See YAY-man-den fuer Re-pa-ra-TOO-ren aufs TSI-mer SHI-kken?

I'm locked out of my room, could you unlock it?
Ich habe mich selbst aus dem Zimmer ausgesperrt, können Sie es wieder öffnen?
Ikh HAH-be mikh selbst aus daym TSI-mer AUS-ge-shperrt, KOE-nen See es VEE-der OEFF-nen?

Our door is jammed and won't open.
Unsere Tür klemmt und geht nicht auf.
Un-se-re Tuer klemmt oond gayt nikht auf.

How do you work the shower?
Wie funktioniert die Dusche?
Vee funnk-tsee-o-NEERT dee DOO-she?

Are the consumables in the room free?
Sind die Verbrauchsartikel im Zimmer im Preis inbegriffen?
Sind dee Fer-BRAUKHS-ar-TEE-kel im TSI-mer im Prighs IN-be-grif-fen?

What is my final bill for the stay, including incidentals?
Wie hoch ist meine Endabrechnung, einschließlich der Nebenkosten?
Vee hohkh ist MIGH-ne END-ab-rekh-noong, IGHN-shleess-likh der NAY-ben-kos-ten?

Can you show me to my room?
Können Sie mir den Weg zu meinem Zimmer zeigen?
KOE-nen See meer den Vayg tsoo MIGH-nem TSI-mer TSIGH-gen?

Where can I get ice for my room?
Wo bekomme ich Eis für mein Zimmer?
Voh be-KOM-me ikh Ighs fuer mighn TSI-mer?

Do you have any rooms available?
Haben Sie noch freie Zimmer?
HAH-ben See nokh FRIGH-e TSI-mer?

Do you sell bottled water?
Verkaufen Sie Wasserflaschen?
Ver-KAU-fen See VA-sser-flash-en?

Our towels are dirty.
Unsere Handtücher sind schmutzig.
Un-se-re HAND-tue-kher sind SHMOO-tsig.

Have you stayed at this hotel before?
Waren Sie schon einmal in diesem Hotel?
VAH-ren See shohn IGHN-mal in DEE-sem Ho-TEL?

How much is a room for two adults?
Wie viel kostet ein Zimmer für zwei Erwachsene?
Vee feel KOS-tet ighn TSI-mer fuer tsvigh Er-VAKH-se-ne?

Does the room come with a microwave?
Hat das Zimmer eine Mikrowelle?
Hat das TSI-mer IGH-ne MEE-kro-vel-le?

May I see the room first? That way I will know if I like it.
Kann ich das Zimmer sehen? Dann weiß, ich ob ich es nehmen möchte.
Kann ikh das TSI-mer SAY-hen? Dann vighss ikh, ob ikh es NAY-men MOEKH-te.

Do you have a room that is quieter?
Haben Sie ein Zimmer, in dem es leiser ist?
HAH-ben See ighn TSIM-mer, in daym es LIGH-ser ist?

How much is the deposit for my stay?
Wie hoch ist die Kaution?
Vee hohkh ist dee Kau-tsee-OHN?

Is the tap water drinkable at the hotel?
Kann man das Leitungswasser im Hotel trinken?
Kann man das LIGH-toongs-vas-ser im Ho-TEL TRIN-ken?

Will there be any holds on my credit card?
Wird auf meiner Kreditkarte ein bestimmter Betrag reserviert?
Vird auf MIGH-ner Kre-DEET-kar-te ighn be-SHTIMM-ter Be-TRAHG re-ser-VEERT?

156

Can I get a replacement room key?
Kann ich einen zweiten Schlüssel für das Zimmer haben?
Kann ikh IGH-nen TSVIGH-ten SHLUE-sel fuer das TSI-mer HAH-ben?

How much is a replacement room key?
Wie viel kostet ein Nachschlüssel?
Vee feel KOS-stet ighn NAKH-shlues-sel?

Does the bathroom have a shower or a bathtub?
Hat das Badezimmer eine Dusche oder eine Badewanne?
Hat das BAH-de-tsim-mer IGH-ne DOO-she OH-der IGH-ne BAH-de-van-ne?

Are any of the channels on the TV available in English?
Gibt es irgendwelche englischen Fernsehsender?
Geebt es IR-gend-vel-khe ENG-lish-en FERN-say-sen-der?

I want a bigger room.
Ich brauche ein größeres Zimmer.
Ikh BRAU-ckhe ighn GROE-sse-res TSI-mer.

Do you serve breakfast in the morning?
Gibt es Frühstück?
Geebt es FRUE-shtuek?

Oh, it's spacious.
Oh, es ist groß.
Oh, es ist grohss.

My room is this way.
Mein Zimmer ist dort.
Mighn TSI-mer ist dort.

Straight down the hall.
Den Flur hinunter.
Den Floor hee-NUN-ter.

Can you suggest a different hotel?
Können Sie ein anderes Hotel empfehlen?
KOE-nen See ighn AN-de-res Ho-TEL em-PFAY-len?

Does the room have a safe for my valuables?
Hat das Zimmer einen Safe für meine Wertsachen?
Hat das TSI-mer IGH-nen Sayf fuer MIGH-ne VAYRT-sa-khen?

Please clean my room.
Bitte reinigen Sie mein Zimmer.
BI-te RIGH-nee-gen See mighn TSI-mer.

Don't disturb me, please.
Bitte stören Sie mich nicht.
BI-te STOE-ren See mikh nikht.

Can you wake me up at noon?
Können Sie mich gegen Mittag aufwecken?
KOE-nen See mikh GAY-gen MI-tag AUF-vek-ken?

I would like to check out of my hotel room.
Ich möchte gerne auschecken.
Ikh MOEKH-te GAYR-ne AUS-tshek-ken.

Please increase the cleanup duty of my hotel room.
Bitte sorgen Sie für mehr Sauberkeit in meinem Hotelzimmer.
BI-te SOR-gen See fuer mayr SAU-ber-kight in MIGH-nem Ho-TEL-tsi-mer.

Is the Marriott any good?
Ist das Marriott gut?
Ist das MAE-ree-ot goot?

Is it expensive to stay at the Marriott?
Ist es teuer, im Marriott abzusteigen?
Ist es TOY-er, im MAE-ree-ot AB-tsoo-shtigh-gen?

I think our room has bedbugs.
Ich glaube, unser Zimmer hat Bettwanzen.
Ikh GLAU-be, UN-ser TSI-mer hat BETT-van-tsen.

Can you send an exterminator to our room?
Können Sie einen Kammerjäger in mein Zimmer schicken?
KOE-nen See IGH-nen KAM-mer-yae-ger in main TSI-mer SHIK-ken?

I need to speak to your manager.
Ich muss mit Ihrem Manager sprechen.
Ikh muss mit EE-rem MAE-nae-dsher SHPRAY-khen.

Do you have the number to corporate?
Haben Sie die Nummer der Geschäftsleitung?
HAH-ben See dee NUM-mer der Ge-SHAEFTS-ligh-toong?

Does the hotel shuttle go to the casino?
Fährt das Hotel-Shuttle zum Kasino?
Faert das Ho-TEL-Sha-tel tsoom Ka-SEE-no?

Can you call me when the hotel shuttle is on its way?
Können Sie mir Bescheid geben, sobald das Hotel-Shuttle unterwegs ist?
KOE-nen See meer Be-SHIGHD GAY-eben, so-BALD das Ho-TEL-Sha-tel un-ter-VAYGS ist?

Can we reserve this space for a party?
Können wir dieses Areal für eine Party reservieren?
KOE-nen veer DEE-ses A-re-AHL fuer IGH-ne PAR-tee re-ser-VEE-ren?

What is the guest limit for reserving an area?
Wie viele Gäste können wir maximal in ein Areal einladen?
Vee FEE-le GAES-te KOE-nen veer MAK-see-mahl in ighn Ah-re-AHL IGHN-lah-den?

What are the rules for reserving an area?
Was sind die Regeln für die Reservierung eines Areals?
Vas sind dee RAY-geln fuer dee Re-ser-VEE-roong IGH-nes Ah-re-AHLS?

Can we serve or drink alcohol during our get together?
Dürfen wir bei der Feier Alkohol ausschenken und trinken?
DUER-fen veer bigh der FIGH-er AL-ko-hohl AUS-shen-ken oond TRIN-ken?

I would like to complain about a noisy room next to us.
Ich möchte mich über einen lauten Nachbarn beschweren.
Ikh MOEKH-te mikh UE-ber IGH-nen LAU-ten NAKH-barn be-SHVAY-ren.

We have some personal items missing from our room.
Einige unserer persönlichen Gegenstände aus dem Zimmer sind verschwunden.
IGH-nee-ge UN-ser-er per-SOEN-lee-khen GAY-gen-SHTAEN-de aus dem TSI-mer sind fer-SHVUN-den.

SPORTS AND EXERCISE

Can we walk faster?
Können wir schneller gehen?
KOE-nen veer SHNEL-ler GAY-hen?

Do you want to go to a drag race track?
Möchten Sie zu einer Drag-Race-Strecke mitkommen?
MOEKH-ten See tsoo IGH-ner DRAEG-Race-Shtrek-ke MIT-kom-men?

Are you taking a walk?
Gehen Sie spazieren?
GAY-hen See shpa-TSEE-ren?

Do you want to jog for a kilometer or two?
Wollen Sie ein bis zwei Kilometer joggen?
VOL-len See ighn bis tsvigh KEE-loh-may-ter DSHOG-gen?

How about fast walking?
Wie wäre es mit schnellem Gehen?
Vee VAE-re es mit SHNEL-lem GAY-hen?

Would you like to walk with me?
Möchten Sie mit mir zu Fuß gehen?
MOEKH-ten See mit meer tsoo Foos GAY-hen?

He is a really good player.
Er ist ein wirklich guter Spieler.
Er ist ighn VIRK-likh GOO-ter SHPEE-ler.

I feel bad that they traded him to the other team.
Ich finde es schade, dass er zum anderen Team gewechselt ist.
Ikh FIN-de es SHAH-de, dass er tsoom AN-de-ren Teem ge-VEKH-selt ist.

Did you see that home run?
Haben Sie diesen Home Run gesehen?
HAH-ben See DEE-sen Home Run ge-SAY-hen?

I have been a fan of that team for many years.
Ich bin schon jahrelang ein Fan dieses Teams.
Ikh bin shohn YAH-re-lang ighn Faen DEE-ses Teems.

Who is your favorite team?
Welches ist Ihr Lieblings-Team?
VEL-khes ist Eer LEEB-lings-teem?

Pelé is my favorite player.
Pelé ist mein Lieblings-Spieler.
Pe-LE ist mighn LEEB-lings-shpee-ler.

Do you like soccer?
Mögen Sie Fußball?
MOE-gen See FOOSS-ball?

Do you watch American football?
Schauen Sie American Football?
SHAU-en See A-MAY-ree-kan FOOT-bohl?

Are there any games on right now?
Werden gerade irgendwelche Spiele gezeigt?
VER-den ge-RAH-de IR-gend-vel-khe SHPEE-le ge-TSIGHT?

That was a bad call by the ref.
Das war eine schlechte Schiedsrichterentscheidung.
Das vahr IGH-ne SHLEKH-te SHEEDS-rikh-ter-ent-SHIGH-doong.

I put a lot of money on this game.
Ich habe viel Geld auf dieses Spiel gesetzt.
Ikh HAH-be feel Geld auf DEE-ses Shpeel ge-SETST.

His stats have been incredible this season.
Seine Statistiken waren hervorragend in dieser Saison.
SIGH-ne Shtah-TIS-tee-ken VAH-ren her-FOHR-rah-gend in dee-ser Sigh-SOHN.

Do you want to play baseball today?
Wollen Sie heute Baseball spielen?
VOL-len See HOY-te BAES-bohl SHPEE-len?

Let's go to the soccer field and practice.
Lass uns auf den Fußballplatz trainieren gehen.
Lass uns auf den FOOS-ball-plats trai-NEE-ren GAY-hen.

I am barely working up a sweat.
Ich schwitze fast gar nicht.
Ikh SHVI-tse fast gahr nikht.

Let's go to the gym and lift weights.
Lass uns ins Fitnessstudio Gewichtheben gehen.
Lass uns ins FIT-ness-SHTOO-dee-o Ge-VIKHT-hay-ben GAY-hen.

Give me more weights.
Geben Sie mir mehr Gewichte.
GAY-ben See meer mayr Ge-VIKH-te.

Take some weights off.
Nehmen Sie etwas Gewicht herunter.
NAY-men See ET-vas Ge-VIKHT he-ROON-ter.

Will you spot me?
Können Sie mir Hilfestellung leisten?
KOE-nen See meer HIL-fe-shtel-loong LIGHS-ten?

How long do you want me to run on the treadmill?
Wie lange soll ich auf dem Laufband laufen?
Vee LAN-ge soll ikh auf dem LAUF-band LAU-fen?

Is this the best gym in the area?
Ist das das beste Fitnessstudio in der Gegend?
Ist das das BES-te FIT-ness-SHTOO-dee-o in dayr GAY-gend?

Do I need a membership to enter this gym?
Brauche ich für dieses Fitnessstudio eine Mitgliedschaft?
BRAU-khe ikh fuer DEE-ses FIT-ness-SHTOO-dee-o IGH-ne MIT-gleed-shaft?

Do you have trial memberships for tourists?
Gibt es eine Test-Mitgliedschaft für Touristen?
Geebt es IGH-ne TEST-mit-gleed-shaft fuer Too-RIS-sten?

My muscles are still sore from the last workout.
Meine Muskeln tun immer noch vom letzten Training weh.
MIGH-ne MOOS-keln toon IM-mer nokh fom LET-sten TRAE-ning vay.

Give me a second while I adjust this.
Geben Sie mir eine Sekunde, damit ich das einstellen kann.
GAY-ben See meer IGH-ne Se-KOON-de, da-MIT ikh das IGHN-shtel-len kann.

Time to hit the steam room!
Zeit für das Dampfbad!
Tsight fuer das DAMPF-bahd!

You can put that in my locker.
Sie können das in meinen Spind legen.
See KOE-nen das in migh-nen Shpind LAY-gen.

I think we have to take turns on this machine.
Ich glaube, wir müssen uns bei diesem Gerät abwechseln.
Ikh GLAU-be, veer MUE-sen uns bigh DEE-sem Ge-RAET AB-wekh-seln.

Make sure to wipe down the equipment when you are done.
Bitte säubern Sie das Equipment, wenn Sie fertig sind.
BI-te SOY-bern See das E-KVIP-ment, wenn See FER-tig seend.

Is there a time limit on working out here?
Gibt es hier ein Zeitlimit für das Training?
Geebt es heer ighn TSIGHT-li-mit fuer das TRAE-ning?

We should enter a marathon.
Wir sollten einen Marathon laufen.
Veer SOLL-ten IGH-nen MA-ra-ton LAU-fen.

How has your diet been going?
Wie läuft deine Diät?
Vee loyft DIGH-ne Dee-AET?

Are you doing keto?
Machen Sie Keto?
MA-khen See KAY-to?

Make sure to stay hydrated while you work out.
Trinken Sie genug, wenn Sie trainieren.
TRIN-ken See ge-NOOG, venn See trae-NEE-ren.

I'll go grab you a protein shake.
Ich bringe Ihnen einen Protein-Shake.
Ikh BRIN-ge EE-nen IGH-nen Pro-tae-EEN-Shaek.

Do you want anything else? I'm buying.
Möchten Sie noch etwas anderes? Ich zahle.
MOEKH-ten See nokh ET-vas AN-de-res? Ikh TSAH-le.

I need to buy some equipment before I play that.
Ich brauche etwas mehr Equipment, bevor ich das spielen kann.
Ikh BRAU-khe ET-vas mayr E-KVIP-ment, be-FOHR ikh das SHPEE-len kann.

Do you want to spar?
Wollen Sie kämpfen?
VOL-len See KAEM-pfen?

Full contact sparring.
Vollkontakt-Kampf.
FOLL-kon-takt-Kampf.

Just a simple practice round.
Nur zum Training.
Noor tsoom TRAE-ning.

Do you want to wrestle?
Wollen Sie ringen?
VOL-len See RING-en?

What are the rules to play this game?
Welche Regeln gelten in diesem Spiel?
VEL-khe RAY-geln GEL-ten in DEE-sem Shpeel?

Do we need a referee?
Brauchen wir einen Schiedsrichter?
BRAU-khen veer IGH-nen SHEEDS-rikh-ter?

I don't agree with that call.
Ich bin nicht einverstanden mit der Entscheidung.
Ikh bin nikht IGHN-fer-SHTAN-den mit der Ent-SHIGH-doong.

Can we get another opinion on that score?
Können wir eine zweite Meinung zu dem Punkt bekommen?
KOE-nen veer IGH-ne TSVIGH-te MIGH-noong tsoo dem Poonkt be-KOM-men?

How about a game of table tennis?
Wie wär's mit Tischtennis?
Vee waers mit TISH-ten-nis?

Do you want to team up?
Spielen wir gemeinsam?
SHPEE-len veer ge-MIGHN-sam?

Goal!
Tor!
Tohr!

Homerun!
Homerun!
Ho-me-run!

Touchdown!
Touchdown!
Touch-down!

Score!
Punkt!
Poonkt!

On your mark, get set, go!
Auf die Plätze, fertig, los!
Auf dee PLAE-tse, FER-tig, lohs!

Do you want to borrow my equipment?
Wollen Sie mein Equipment ausborgen?
VOL-len See mighn E-KVIP-ment AUS-bor-gen?

Hold the game for a second.
Stopp für einen Moment.
Shtopp fuer IGH-nen Mo-MENT.

I don't understand the rules of this game.
Ich verstehe die Regeln des Spiels nicht.
Ikh fer-SHTAY-he dee RAY-geln des Shpeels nikht.

Timeout!
Unterbrechung!
Un-ter-BREKH-oong!

Can we switch sides?
Können wir Seiten wechseln?
KOE-nen veer SIGH-ten VEKH-seln?

There is something wrong with my equipment.
Etwas stimmt nicht mit meinem Equipment.
ET-vas shtimmt nikht mit MIGH-nem E-KVIP-ment.

How about another game?
Noch ein Spiel?
Nokh ighn Shpeel?

I would like a do over of that last game.
Ich möchte eine Revanche.
Ikh MOEKH-te IGH-ne Re-VAUGHN-she.

Do you want to go golfing?
Möchten Sie Golf spielen?
MOEKH-ten See Golf SHPEE-len?

Where can we get a golf cart?
Wo können wir einen Golfwagen bekommen?
Voh KOE-nen veer IGH-nen GOLF-vah-gen be-KOM-men?

Do you have your own clubs?
Haben Sie Ihre eigenen Schläger?
HAH-ben See EE-re IGH-ge-en SHLAE-ger?

Would you like to play with my spare clubs?
Wollen Sie mit meinen Schlägern spielen?
VOL-len See mit MIGH-nen SHLAE-gern SPEE-len?

How many holes do you want to play?
Wie viele Löcher wollen Sie spielen?
Vee FEE-le LOE-kher VOL-len See SHPEE-len?

Do I have to be a member of this club to play?
Muss man Club-Mitglied sein, um spielen zu können?
Muss man KLOOB-Mit-gleed sighn, um SHPEE-len tsoo KOE-nen?

Let me ice this down, it is sore.
Lassen Sie mich etwas Eis auflegen, es ist wund.
LAS-sen See mikh ET-was Ighs AUF-le-gen, es ist voond.

I can't keep up with you, slow down.
Ich bin nicht so schnell, bitte etwas langsamer.
Ikh bin nikht soh shnell, BI-te ET-vas LANG-sah-mer.

Let's pick up the pace a little bit.
Etwas schneller, bitte.
ET-vas SHNE-ler, BI-te.

166

Do you need me to help you with that?

Brauchen Sie Hilfe?

BRAU-khen See HIL-fe?

Am I being unfair?

Bin ich unfair?

Bin ikh UN-faer?

Let's switch teams for the next game.

Lass uns für das nächste Spiel die Teams tauschen.

Lass uns fuer das NAEKH-te Shpeel dee Teems TAU-shen.

Hand me those weights.

Bitte geben Sie mir diese Gewichte.

BI-te GAY-ben See meer DEE-se Ge-VIKH-te.

THE FIRST 24 HOURS AFTER ARRIVING

When did you arrive?
Wann sind Sie angekommen?
Vann sind See AN-ge-kom-men?

That was a very pleasant flight.
Das war ein angenehmer Flug.
Das vahr ighn AN-ge-nay-mer Floog.

Yes, it was a very peaceful trip. Nothing bad happened.
Ja, es war ein angenehmer Flug. Es ist nichts Schlimmes passiert.
Yah, es vahr ighn AN-ge-nay-mer Floog. Es ist nikhts SHLIM-mes pa-SEERT.

I have jetlag so need to lay down for a bit.
Ich habe einen Jetlag, darum muss ich mich ein wenig hinlegen.
Ikh HAH-be IGH-nen JET-lag, DAH-rum muss ikh mikh ighn VAY-nig HIN-lay-gen.

No, that was my first time flying.
Nein, das war mein erster Flug.
Nighn, das vahr mighn ER-ster Floog.

When is the check-in time?
Wann soll ich einchecken?
Vann soll ikh IGHN-dshe-ken?

Do we need to get cash?
Brauchen wir Bargeld?
BRAU-khen veer BAHR-geld?

How much money do you have on you?
Wie viel Bargeld haben Sie mit?
Vee FEEL BAHR-geld HAH-ben See mit?

How long do you want to stay here?
Wie lange wollen Sie hierbleiben?
Vee LAN-ge VOL-len See HEER-bligh-ben?

Do we have all of our luggage?
Haben wir all unser Gepäck?
HAH-ben veer all UN-ser Ge-PAEK?

Let's walk around the city a bit before checking in.
Lass uns ein wenig durch die Stadt gehen, bevor wir einchecken.
Lass uns ighn VAY-nig doorkh dee Shtat GAY-hen, be-FOHR veer IGHN-dshe-ken.

When is check-in time for our hotel?
Wann sollen wir ins Hotel einchecken?
Vann SOL-len veer ins Ho-TEL IGHN-dshe-ken?

I'll call the landlord and let him know we landed.
Ich rufe den Vermieter an und sage ihm, dass wir gelandet sind.
Ikh ROO-fe den Fer-MEE-ter an oond SAH-ge eem, dass veer ge-LAN-det sind.

Let's find a place to rent a car.
Lass uns einen Ort suchen, wo wir ein Auto mieten können.
Lass uns IGH-nen Ort SOO-khen, vo veer ighn AU-to MEE-ten KOE-nen.

Let's walk around the hotel room and make sure it's correct.
Lass uns durch das Hotelzimmer gehen und sichergehen, dass alles passt.
Lass uns doorkh das Ho-TEL-tsi-mer GAY-hen oond SI-kher-gay-hen, dass AL-les passt.

We'll look at our apartment and make sure everything is in order.
Wir sehen uns unsere Wohnung an und kontrollieren, ob alles passt.
Veer SAY-hen uns UN-se-re VOH-noong an oond kon-trol-LEE-ren, ob AL-les passt.

THE LAST 24 HOURS BEFORE LEAVING

Where are the passports?
Wo sind die Pässe?
Voh sind dee PAE-se?

Did you fill out the customs forms?
Haben Sie die Zoll-Formulare ausgefüllt?
HAH-ben See dee TSOLL-For-moo-LAH-re AUS-ge-fuellt?

Make sure to pack everything.
Kontrollieren Sie, ob Sie alles eingepackt haben.
Kon-tro-LEE-ren See, ob See AL-les IGHN-ge-pakt HAH-ben.

Where are we going?
Wohin geht es?
Vo-HIN gayt es?

Which flight are we taking?
Welchen Flug nehmen wir?
VEL-khen Floog NAY-men veer?

Check your pockets.
Kontrollieren Sie Ihre Taschen.
Kon-tro-LEE-ren See EE-re TA-shen.

I need to declare some things for customs.
Ich muss etwas für den Zoll deklarieren.
Ikh muss ET-vas fuer den Tsoll day-kla-REE-ren.

No, I have nothing to declare.
Nein, ich habe nichts zu deklarieren.
NIghn, ikh HAH-be nikhts tsoo day-kla-REE-ren.

What is the checkout time?
Wann soll ich auschecken?
Vann soll ikh AUS-dshe-ken?

Make sure your phone is charged.
Versichern Sie sich, dass Ihr Telefon geladen ist.
Fer-SIKH-ern See sikh, dass Eer TE-le-fon ge-LAH-den eest.

Is there a fee attached to this?
Kostet das extra?
KOS-tet das EKS-tra?

Do we have any outstanding bills to pay?
Haben wir noch Rechnungen zu bezahlen?
HAH-ben veer nokh REKH-nung-en tsoo be-TSAH-len?

What time does our flight leave?
Wann fliegt unser Flugzeug?
Vann fleegt UN-ser FLOOG-tsoyg?

What time do we need to be in the airport?
Wann müssen wir am Flughafen sein?
Vann MUES-sen veer am FLOOG-hah-fen sighn?

How bad is the traffic going in the direction of the airport?
Wie schlimm ist der Verkehr in Richtung Flughafen?
Vee shlimm ist der Fer-KAYR in RIKH-toong FLOOG-hah-fen?

Are there any detours we can take?
Gibt es alternative Wege, die wir nehmen können?
Geebt es al-ter-na-TEE-fe VAY-ge, dee veer NAY-men KOEN-en?

What haven't we seen from our list since we've been down here?
Was von unserer Liste haben wir noch nicht gesehen, seit wir hier sind?
Vas fon UN-ser-er LIS-te HAH-ben veer nokh nikht ge-SAY-hen, sight veer heer sind?

We should really buy some souvenirs here.
Wir sollten hier wirklich einige Souvenirs kaufen.
Veer SOLL-ten heer VIRK-likh IGH-nee-ge Soo-ve-NEERS KAU-fen.

Do you know any shortcuts that will get us there faster?
Kennen Sie eine Abkürzung?
KEN-nen See IGH-ne AB-kuer-tsoong?

GPS the location and save it.
Diesen Ort bitte einspeichern.
DEE-sen Ort BI-te IGHN-shpigh-khern.

Are the items we're bringing back allowed on the plane?
Dürfen wir die Sachen im Flugzeug mitnehmen?
DUER-fen veer DEE-se SA-khen im FLOOG-tsoyg MIT-nay-men?

We should call our families back home before leaving.
Wir sollten unsere Familien zuhause anrufen, bevor wir losfahren.
Veer SOLL-ten UN-se-re Fa-MEE-lee-en tsoo-HAU-se AN-roo-fen, be-FOHR veer LOHS-fah-ren.

Make sure the pet cage is locked.
Stelle bitte sicher, dass der Haustier-Käfig verschlossen ist.
SHTEL-le BI-te SI-kher, dass der HAUS-teer-Kae-fig fer-SHLO-sen ist.

Go through your luggage again
Kontrolliere den Reisekoffer noch einmal.
Kon-trol-LEE-re den RIGH-se-kof-fer nokh IGHN-mal.

CONCLUSION

Congratulations! You have reached the end of this book and learned over **1,500** ways to express yourself in the German language! It is a moment to celebrate, since you are now much closer to achieving complete fluency of the German tongue.

However, the learning simply cannot end here – you may have unlocked a massive amount of incredibly useful day-to-day phrases that will get you anywhere you need to go, but are you prepared to use them correctly? Furthermore, will you actually remember them during your travels when faced with one of the situations we've presented in this book?

Only by continuously studying the material found in these chapters will you ever be able to summon the words and phrases encountered above, since it isn't a matter of *what* the phrases are but *how* and *when* to use them. Knowing the exact context is crucial, as well as reinforcing your knowledge with other materials.

For this reason, we have created a quick list of tips to make the most of this German Phrasebook and expanding your vocabulary and grasp of the German language:

1. **Practice every day:** You can be very good at something thanks to the gift of natural talent, but practice is the only way to *stay* good. Make sure to constantly pick up the book and read the words, saying them out loud and taking note of your mistakes so you can correct them.

2. **Read while listening:** A very popular and modern way of learning a new language is by using the RwL (reading while listening) method. It has been proven that this method can greatly boost fluency, help you ace language tests, and improve your learning in other subjects. Feel free to try out our audiobooks and other listening materials in German – you'll love them!

3. **Studying in groups:** It's always best to go on an adventure together – even if it's a language adventure! You'll enjoy yourself more if you can find someone who wants to learn with you. Look to friends, your partner, your family members, or colleagues for support, and maybe they can even help you make the process easier and quicker!

4. **Creating your own exercises:** This book provides you with plenty of material for your learning processes, and you will probably be happy with reading it every time you can...however, you need to increase the difficulty by looking for other words and phrases in the German language which you don't know the pronunciation to and trying to decipher them for yourself. Use the knowledge you've gained with previous lessons to discover entirely new words!

With that said, we have now fully concluded this German phrase book, which will surely accelerate your learning to new levels. Don't forget to follow every tip we've included and keep an eye out for our additional German materials.

MORE FROM LINGO MASTERY

Have you been trying to learn German and simply can't find the way to expand your vocabulary?

Do your teachers recommend you boring textbooks and complicated stories that you don't really understand?

Are you looking for a way to learn the language quicker without taking shortcuts?

If you answered "Yes!" to at least one of those previous questions, then this book is for you! We've compiled the **2000 Most Common Words in German**, a list of terms that will expand your vocabulary to levels previously unseen.

Did you know that — according to an important study — learning the top two thousand (2000) most frequently used words will enable you to understand up to **84%** of all non-fiction and **86.1%** of fiction literature and **92.7%** of oral speech? Those are amazing stats, and this book will take you even further than those numbers!

In this book:

- A detailed introduction with tips and tricks on how to improve your learning

- A list of 2000 of the most common words in German and their translations
- An example sentence for each word – in both German and English
- Finally, a conclusion to make sure you've learned and supply you with a final list of tips

Don't look any further, we've got what you need right here!

In fact, we're ready to turn you into a German speaker… are you ready to get involved in becoming one?

Do you know what the hardest thing for a German learner is?

Finding PROPER reading material that they can handle...which is precisely the reason we've written this book!

Teachers love giving out tough, expert-level literature to their students, books that present many new problems to the reader and force them to search for words in a dictionary every five minutes — it's not entertaining, useful or motivating for the student at all, and many soon give up on learning at all!

In this book we have compiled 20 easy-to-read, compelling and fun stories that will allow you to expand your vocabulary and give you the tools to improve your grasp of the wonderful German tongue.

How German Short Stories for Beginners works:

- Each story is interesting and entertaining with realistic dialogues and day-to-day situations.
- The summaries follow a synopsis in German and in English of what you just read, both to review the lesson and for you to see if you understood what the tale was about.
- At the end of those summaries, you'll be provided with a list of the most relevant vocabulary involved in the lesson, as well as slang and sayings that you may not have understood at first glance!

- Finally, you'll be provided with a set of tricky questions in German, providing you with the chance to prove that you learned something in the story. Don't worry if you don't know the answer to any — we will provide them immediately after, but no cheating!

We want you to feel comfortable while learning the tongue; after all, no language should be a barrier for you to travel around the world and expand your social circles!

So look no further! Pick up your copy of German Short Stories for Beginners and start learning German right now!

This book has been written by a native German author and is recommended for A2+ level learners.

Is conversational German turning a little too tricky for you? Do you have no idea how to order a meal or book a room at a hotel?

If your answer to any of the previous questions was 'Yes', then this book is for you!

If there's even been something tougher than learning the grammar rules of a new language, it's finding the way to speak with other people in that tongue. Any student knows this – we can try our best at practicing, but you always want to avoid making embarrassing mistakes or not getting your message through correctly.

"How do I get out of this situation?" many students ask themselves, to no avail, but no answer is forthcoming.

Until now.

We have compiled **MORE THAN ONE HUNDRED** conversational German stories for beginners along with their translations, allowing new German speakers to have the necessary tools to begin studying how to set a meeting, rent a car or tell a doctor that they don't feel well. We're not wasting time here with conversations that don't go anywhere: if you want to know how to solve problems (while learning a ton of German along the way, obviously), this book is for you!

How Conversational German Dialogues works:

- Each new chapter will have a fresh, new story between two people who wish to solve a common, day-to-day issue that you will surely encounter in real life.
- An German version of the conversation will take place first, followed by an English translation. This ensures that you fully understood just what it was that they were saying.
- Before and after the main section of the book, we shall provide you with an introduction and conclusion that will offer you important strategies, tips and tricks to allow you to get the absolute most out of this learning material.
- That's about it! Simple, useful and incredibly helpful; you will NOT need another conversational German book once you have begun reading and studying this one!

We want you to feel comfortable while learning the tongue; after all, no language should be a barrier for you to travel around the world and expand your social circles!

So look no further! Pick up your copy of Conversational German Dialogues and start learning German right now!

Made in the USA
Middletown, DE
21 February 2021